THE KID'S GUIDE TO LOS ANGELES COUNTY

THE
K I D'S
GUIDE TO
LOS ANGELES
COUNTY

1st
edition

Eileen Ogint

gpp®
travel

Guilford, Connecticut

Thank you to Meghan McCloskey and Jonathan Boydston for their research help and
Melissa Miller for contributing the games. Thank you to all the young people who
contributed their travel tips, especially to Los Angeles native Christopher Morales
who gathered all of his friends' suggestions.

All the information in this guidebook is subject to change.
We recommend that you call ahead to obtain current
information before traveling.

To buy books in quantity for corporate use
or incentives, call **(800) 962-0973**
or e-mail **premiums@GlobePequot.com.**

Editor: Amy Lyons
Project Editor: Lauren Brancato
Layout: Maggie Peterson
Text Design: Sheryl Kober
Illustrations licensed by Shutterstock.com

ISBN 978-0-7627-9218-4

Printed in the United States of America
10 9 8 7 6 5 4 3 2 1

Contents

1

City of Angels:
Movies, Tar Pits, Disneyland & Much More

What makes LA different from other cities is how spread out it is.

Greater Los Angeles, or LA for short, is made up of five counties: Los Angeles, Orange, Riverside, San Bernardino, and Ventura. The area stretches from the desert to the sea and the mountains to the valleys.

Where do you think you want to go first?

- Hollywood, the entertainment capital of the world and home to Universal Studios Hollywood?

- The Beach Cities (Manhattan Beach, Hermosa Beach, and Redondo Beach)? Maybe you can try to surf (or at least boogie board)!

A LOCAL KID SAYS:
"I like to see all the cool cars TV stars and movie stars drive."
—Dayne, 11

- Beverly Hills and West Hollywood (maybe you'll see a celebrity on Rodeo Drive)?

- Santa Monica with its pier and Third Street Promenade?

- The Valley, which is home to LA's movie studios?

- The West Side with its famous museums and Original Farmers Market?

The good thing about LA is whatever you like to do—play or watch sports, go shopping, try new foods, go to the beach, see cool museums—you can do it all here!

Do you think you want to be a movie star!? Sure, a lot of people come to Los Angeles to get into the entertainment business, but that wasn't always the case.

A LOCAL KID SAYS:
"My favorite thing to do in LA is to see the city as a whole. The city is alive in the day and at night so you get to see it all!"
—Yan, 15

{ **What's Cool?** Getting lunch from a food truck, whether you want a taco, Korean barbecue, or fried chicken. You can find where the trucks are on the Southern California Mobile Food Vendors Association website (socalmfva.com).

The first settlers were farmers who came here around 1781—at the same time the American Revolution was being fought. Nothing is left of their homes, but walk down **Olvera Street** (W-26 Olvera St., Los Angeles; 213-687-4391; calleolvera.com)—right near where those first farmers lived—and you can see the **Avila Adobe** (10 Olvera St., Los Angeles; 213-485-6855; elpueblo.lacity.org/elpaa1.htm), the oldest existing home in Los Angeles. Olvera Street is a lively Mexican marketplace where you can get everything from a taco to a sombrero.

Stop by the **Plaza Firehouse** (125 Paseo de la Plaza, Ste. 400, Los Angeles; 213-485-6855; elpueblo.lacity.org/elppfh1 .htm)—the first firehouse built in the city—and see the old firefighting tools and trucks.

There are 27 historic build-ings here at the **El Pueblo de Los Angeles Historic Monument.**

Today Los Angeles is a mixture of many cultures and

languages—Hispanic, African American, Japanese, Chinese, and Korean among them. Just a few blocks from Olvera Street is **Little Tokyo**—take a stroll around the **Japanese Village Plaza** (335 E. 2nd St., Los Angeles; 213-617-1900; japanesevillageplaza.net) and learn about the Japanese-American experience at the **Japanese American National Museum** (100 N. Central Ave., Los Angeles; 213-625-0414; janm.org). There is also **Chinatown** (North Broadway at North Hill Street, Downtown, Los Angeles; 213-680-0243; chinatownla .com). If you are here during Chinese New Year, you can catch **The Golden Dragon Parade** that celebrates this holiday in Chinatown (lachinesechamber.org).

A VISITING KID SAYS:
"Get a Japanese umbrella from Little Tokyo."
—Shaelynn, 10, San Diego, CA

Check out the **Cathedral of Our Lady of the Angels** (555 W. Temple St., Los Angeles; 213-680-5200; olacathedral.org). It looks like a fortress, but it is actually a big church—in fact, it's one of the world's largest cathedrals. **The Walt Disney Concert Hall** (111 S. Grand Ave., Los Angeles; 323-850-2000; laphil.com/philpedia/about-walt-disney-concert-hall) is not only the home of the LA Philharmonic orchestra, but it is also a very famous building. You can take a free tour!

Have you heard of the famous **Staples Center** (1111 S. Figueroa St., Los Angeles; 213-742-7326; staples center.com) where the LA Lakers, Clippers, and Sparks basketball teams play? A lot of famous musicians play here too. Doesn't it look like a flying saucer?

Right across the street from the **Staples Center** is **L.A. Live** (800 W. Olympic Blvd., Los Angeles; 213-763-5483; lalive.com) with a huge theater, megaplex movie theater, and more, including the **Grammy Museum** (800 W. Olympic Blvd., A245, Los Angeles; 213-765-6800; grammy museum.org). Grammy trophies are the top awards for music. Here you can try your hand at mixing and rapping.

There is a lot to see downtown! (Let's not forget **City Hall:** 200 N. Spring St., Los Angeles; 213-978-1059; lacity hall.org—on clear days you can see all around from the observation deck).

{ **What's Cool?** The 90 blocks of southwestern downtown are famous for fashionistas and bargain hunters. Check out fashiondistrict.org. You'll find clothes and neat things for kids between 12th Street and Pico Boulevard and designer knockoffs on Santee Alley between Santee Street, Maple Avenue, Olympic Boulevard, and 12th Street. Visit dailycandy.com/los-angeles to find out the latest pint-size trends.

Staying Safe on Vacation

- Write down the name and phone number of the hotel where you are staying.

- Also, write down your parents' phone numbers—or put them in your phone. Carry this record with you wherever you go sightseeing.

A LOCAL KID SAYS:
"I see celebrities often because many of their kids go to our school. They are just regular people."
—Max, 12

- Never approach a vehicle unless you know the owner and are accompanied by an adult.

- Practice "what-if" situations with your parents. What should you do if you get lost in a museum? On a city street? Who should you ask for help?

- Wherever you are, decide on a central, easy-to-locate spot to meet in case you get separated.

- Only ask uniformed people for help if you get lost— police officers, firefighters, store security guards or store clerks, or museum officials wearing official badges or identification badges.

Grammy Museum

Love music? You'll love the Grammy Museum in downtown LA, which houses four floors of exhibits all about the art and technology of the recording process. You can explore nearly 160 different kinds of music—songs and stories—and musical traditions—pop, folk, classical, jazz, and more. Check out the touch screens that help you see where the sounds of American music have come from and how they have changed. The best part is the chance to make your own music just like in a real studio; you'll hear what you created! You can even play electronic musical instruments. There's a lot about the Grammy Awards too. Think you could get nominated some day? (800 W. Olympic Blvd., A245, Los Angeles; 213-765-6800; grammymuseum.org)

A VISITING KID SAYS:
"My favorite museum in LA is the Grammy Museum. I like looking at all the clothing that previous pop stars wore."
—Meghan 13, Taiwan

A LA Holiday Celebration Not to Miss

An 8-square-block neighborhood comes alive every holiday season when the residents put on a display of lights, elves, artificial snow, and more. **Woodland Hills' Candy Cane Lane** is a free event and has been an annual tradition for 60 years, running from the second Saturday in December until the end of the year. (Lubao and Oxnard Streets in Woodland Hills; 818-347-4737; woodlandhillscc.net/candy_cane_lane.html)

DID YOU KNOW?

You can download self-guided walking tour podcasts at downtownlawalks.com.

The statue of Our Lady of the Angels in the Cathedral of Our Lady of the Angels is 8 feet high.

The organ at the Walt Disney Concert Hall has more than 6,000 pipes, some as big as 32 feet!

TELL THE ADULTS:

There is a lot to do that's free in LA:

- Downtown LA offers free summer performances at California Plaza (350 S. Grand Ave., Ste. A-4, Los Angeles; 213-687-2159; grandperformances.org/gp/homepage.html) all summer, while the Pershing Square Summer Concert Series (532 S. Olive St., Los Angeles; 213-847-4970; laparks.org/pershing square) promotes lunchtime Wednesday concerts and special kids events.

- Step into a movie star's footprints at TCL Chinese Theatre (formerly Grauman's Chinese Theatre).

- Wander around Chinatown.

- Volunteer to plant trees around LA with Treepeople (12601 Mulholland Dr., Beverly Hills; 818-753-4600; treepeople.org). This LA-based nonprofit organization has helped spearhead the ecotourism industry by offering numerous opportunities for visitors to volunteer. For more than 30 years, Treepeople has helped plant and care for trees while educating people about the environment.

- Stargaze at Griffith Observatory (2800 E. Observatory Ave., Los Angeles; 213-473-0800; griffithobs.org). To learn about stars that are truly out of this world, the exhibitions and displays in the renovated Griffith Park (4730 Crystal Springs Dr., Los Angeles; 323-913-4688; laparks .org/dos/parks/griffithpk) landmark are all free, as is an introductory video about the building and its contents.

- Drive along the Pacific Coast Highway, which locals call PCH, past some of the best beaches in California and awesome cliffs. In winter, you might see migrating gray whales!

A LOCAL KID SAYS:
"It is amazing to live somewhere where it never really gets cold. You never have to worry about the weather ruining your plans!"
—Anna, 14

Tournament of Roses

It started in 1890 as a New Year's Day celebration with a small procession of flower-covered horses and buggies and an afternoon of races, polo matches, and tug-of-war games. The idea—thought up by some former Easterners and Midwesterners—was to showcase the warm weather.

All the flowers prompted the name: **The Tournament of Roses** (tournamentofroses.com). By 1916, football was a permanent part of the celebration. The Rose Bowl Stadium was built to host the game.

Today, the Tournament of Roses is watched by millions around the world. People who come to Pasadena even camp out to ensure finding a good spot to watch from. It is something to see. Today, the Rose Parade features nearly 50 flower-covered floats—the most delicate flowers are placed in individual vials of water, set in the float one by one. The parade features nearly 20 equestrian units and some 20 marching bands. Work starts on next year's floats nearly as soon as the parade is over.

DID YOU KNOW?

Each float in the Tournament of Roses Parade (tournamentofroses .com) must be entirely covered with natural plants and flowers.

The Metro

The quickest way to get between downtown and Hollywood is on the subway. Contrary to what many think, you can get to just about every corner of Greater LA without a car on subways, light-rail lines, and buses. In fact, the Los Angeles County Metropolitan Transportation Authority—everyone calls it the **Metro**—is one of the biggest in the country. Every day, the Metro efficiently transports hundreds of thousands of passengers throughout LA via subway trains, light-rail, and buses. Metro Rail is LA's rapid transit rail system, with six lines serving 80 stations across the county. The Metro Blue Line connects Long Beach and LA, while the Metro Green Line runs between Norwalk and Redondo Beach. The Metro Red Line subway services downtown, Hollywood, and the San Fernando Valley. The Metro Purple Line runs between Union Station, Wilshire Boulevard, and Western Avenue. The Metro Gold Line runs from Pasadena to East LA. The Metro Expo Line runs between Culver City and downtown. Check out all of the public art! (metro.net; 323-466-3876)

Souvenir Smarts

Located in the oldest part of downtown LA, Olvera Street Market is a famous Mexican marketplace and is a great place to get a taco—or buy souvenirs, as is Chinatown. Before you go souvenir hunting:

- Talk to your parents about how much you can spend. Some families save loose change in a jar all year to spend on souvenirs!

- Consider if you want one big souvenir or several smaller things to add to a collection like pins, patches for your backpack, or stickers that you could put on your water bottle.

- Resist impulse buys and choose something that you can only find in LA.

I ♥ LA

A VISITING KID SAYS:
"Hit the LIDS Store. I got an LA Dodgers cap."
—Josh, 13, Birmingham, AL

Draw what you saw today!

2

Learning About Los Angeles

Through Its Fabulous Museums

Name the place in Los Angeles

where you can time travel from when dinosaurs roamed the earth to when astronauts rocket into space. When you return, you can take a breather to smell the roses or even see a concert.

We're talking about **Exposition Park** (700 Exposition Park Dr.; Los Angeles; 213-744-7458; expositionpark.org). This park is home to the **California Science Center** (700 State Dr., Los Angeles; 213-724-3623; californiascience center.org); the **space shuttle *Endeavour*;** the **Natural History Museum of Los Angeles County** (900 Exposition Blvd., Los Angeles; 213-763-3466; nhm.org) with its huge Dinosaur Hall; the **California African American Museum** (600 State Dr., Los Angeles; 213-744-7432; caamuseum.org); an IMAX theater; the **LA Memorial Coliseum and Sports Arena** (3911 S. Figueroa St., Los Angeles; 213-747-7111; lacoliseumlive.com); and the famous **Exposition Park Rose Garden** (701 State Dr., Los Angeles; 213-763-0114;

laparks.org/exporosegarden/rosegarden.htm).

You may even learn a little LA history while you are at the Becoming Los Angeles exhibit at the Natural History Museum of Los Angeles County. It's got the biggest and most important collection of objects from historic LA—from the early Mexican settlers to the movie business, early cars, and even the animation stand Walt Disney built in his uncle's garage. You can learn the role African Americans played in California's history and in the history of this country nearby at the California African American Museum.

The hard part is knowing where to start, especially when visiting the Natural History Museum.

Make sure to visit the megamouth, the world's

> A LOCAL KID SAYS:
> "The Natural History Museum and the California Space Center are my favorite museums in LA. The space shuttle is cool!"
> —Dylan, 11

DID YOU KNOW?

The LA Memorial Coliseum and Sports Arena in Exposition Park is the only venue in the world to have hosted two Olympics, two Super Bowls, and the World Series. Four million people visit every year.

rarest shark—he's 14.5 feet long and one of only 17 of his kind that have ever been found.

Are you brave enough to stare a wild animal in the face? You can at the African Mammal Hall with dioramas that re-create the animals' natural habitats, from desert to rain forest. Have you ever seen an Arabian oryx or a greater kudu?

The Age of Mammals exhibit tells a story that takes 65 million years. Did you know this museum is the first to trace the evolution of mammals (that includes us!) from the extinction of dinosaurs to the rise of humans? This is also the place to learn about the impact of climate change.

Love creepy-crawlies? Did you know there are about 1.5 million separate species of insects, and there are still millions that haven't been discovered? Check out the spiders and the beetles that create their own waterproof jackets from wax.

If you like sparkly things, you'll love the Gem and Mineral Hall with more than 2,000 stones from around the world. Have you ever touched a meteorite? Seen 300 pounds of gold? You can here. Make sure to save time for the Discovery Center where there's plenty

A LOCAL KID SAYS:
"I see a celebrity at least once a week."
—Jack, 12

more for you to touch and explore. Do you know where a bird's knee bends? You can find out in the Ralph Schreiber Hall of Birds. Check out the species local to Southern California—all 400 of them!

Hope you aren't tired yet because there's still a lot to see at the California Science Center, starting outside in the Science Plaza, which is designed to make you think about the connection between art and science. Check out the Discovery Pavers with words and images sandblasted onto the stones. Each paver is made from a 60-pound slab of granite. Can you answer a riddle on one of them? Check out the California Bench. California's waterways are carved right into the surface of the California-shaped bench.

Just inside is the Science Court (right inside), with all kinds of science demonstrations, air and space exhibits, and even a bike you can ride 3 stories above the ground. Here's your chance to climb up the Cliff Climb.

A lot of people are coming to the Science Center to

A VISITING KID SAYS:
"I liked seeing the giant kelp forest and all the aquariums at the California Science Center."
—Shaelynn, 10, San Diego, CA

see the space shuttle *Endeavour* because it is new here. You can learn a lot about space exploration.

This Science Center is the place to see how and why everything is connected—plants, animals, people, water, and the weather. You can check out some of the world's harshest environments in the Ecosystems exhibit and even get splashed at the River Zone. Check out the Rot Room to see how the breaking down of once living materials helps make the soil ready for new life.

In the Creative World exhibit, you can move a vehicle by turning fuel into motion and take a trip down the Life Tunnel in the World of Life exhibit. Want to catch a ride on a red blood cell and get a tour through your circulatory system? It's crazy!

The great thing about Exposition Park: There is so much to see and do that you can't possibly get bored.

Don't wait for a rainy day.

DID YOU KNOW?

The neck of a mamenchisaurus is longer than a city bus—68 feet. You can walk underneath it at the Natural History Museum of Los Angeles County.

After nearly becoming extinct, over 200 condors now soar over California and neighboring areas. But they still face severe threats.

DINO Power

Did you ever want to play with a dinosaur friend?

At the Natural History Museum of Los Angeles County, you can meet Hunter T. rex and Dakota the triceratops.

Here's your chance to get up close and personal with dinos. They perform each week! Well, not a real dino, but *T. rex* and triceratops puppets that are huge and seem real during Dinosaur Encounters at the Natural History Museum of Los Angeles County.

The Dinosaur Hall at the Natural History Museum has more than 300 real fossils. You'll love how close you can get to them! Check out the *T. rex* series of a trio of different aged dinos.

Check out the dinosaur preparation process in the Level 2 Dino Lab where the staff works on preparing the fossils. Sneak a peek at real fossils and see staff carrying out the day-to-day details of museum work. Everything you see in the lab is real. And, in case you're itching to make firsthand contact with some of these incredible fossils yourself, you can in the discovery area.

Have you ever stepped into a real dinosaur footprint?

ENDEAVOUR

Have you ever wondered how you go to the bathroom in space? You can see a space potty—officially called a Waste Collection System—in the Samuel Oschin Air and Space Center at the California Science Center where the space shuttle *Endeavour* now resides, coming full circle since it was built in Southern California in the 20th century. It completed 25 missions to space! *Endeavour* also carried the first African-American astronaut, Mae Jemison, into space.

Touch *Endeavour*'s tires and check out the galley where the astronauts cooked and ate. Check out the SPACE HAB—at first it was supposed to be for tourists to travel in space, but it ended up being used to give astronauts extra room to work and live. On many missions, it was where scientists put equipment that was going to the *International Space Station,* and it also carried experiments for scientists. Do you think you would want to live and work in space?

{ **What's Cool?** Putting on wings and seeing how it feels to fly at the California Science Center.

EARTHQUAKES

You can feel the shaking of an earthquake during the Earthquake Experience at the California Science Center and build your own structures to see if they would last during a real earthquake.

Earthquakes are caused by very powerful movements of the slabs of rocks making up the earth's crust called tectonic plates. California has many earthquakes because it sits on top of the San Andreas Fault—a crack in the earth that is 10 miles deep in some places. The fault is where two of the world's biggest tectonic plates come together, and when they move, we sometimes feel that as an earthquake.

Here's what you should do if you are caught in an earthquake:

- Stay indoors! Go under a desk or table or stand in a corner. In a high-rise building, get away from windows.

- Don't use elevators.

- If you are outside, get into the open away from trees, buildings, and power lines.

- Be prepared for aftershocks—the smaller shakes that follow the first and biggest quake.

- Stay calm and help others.

TELL THE ADULTS:

Museums are a great place to learn, as well as have fun and meet local families. Here's how to make the most of your experience:

- Take a virtual tour of the museum you plan to visit ahead of time. Because many museums are too big to see in a few hours, zero in on a few exhibits you want to see and don't worry about not getting to everything. You may find online games for the kids like at the California Science Center Fun Lab (californiasciencecenter.org) that will help prepare them for what they are going to see.

- Visit when you are well rested and have eaten. Wear comfortable shoes.

DID YOU KNOW?

Astronauts eat tortillas instead of bread because tortillas don't crumble. Bread crumbs are bad because they could float around or get stuck in an astronaut's eye.

Endeavour is the only spacecraft named by schoolchildren. You can see it at the California Science Center.

- Look on the museum website or ask when you arrive to see if there are special family activities that day.

- Stop at the museum gift shop when you arrive and get some postcards so you can have a scavenger hunt while you explore the galleries, and stop in again on your way out for souvenirs.

- Check out the interactive discovery areas designed for kids, like at the different exhibits in the California Science Center and Natural History Museum of Los Angeles County.

What's Cool? Touching a toe bone of a *T. rex*—real fossils that are 66 and 120 million years old at the Natural History Museum of Los Angeles County.

3
Saber-Toothed Tigers & the La Brea Tar Pits

They wandered into the sticky

asphalt pools that had been softened by the sun and camouflaged by leaves—tiny insects, birds, wolves, saber-toothed cats, and horses. By the time they realized they were stuck, it was too late. They were trapped and would soon die. Many more animals, hoping to feed off of them, would follow and become stuck themselves. So would vultures and condors.

This pattern repeated itself for more than 40,000 years at Rancho La Brea, forming layer after layer of asphalt, fossils, and sediment. Imagine layers of paper and glue with sticks and leaves in between.

A LOCAL KID SAYS:

"My favorite museum in LA is at the La Brea Tar Pits. I like to walk around and see all the fossils in the tar."

—Michaela, 12

Crude oil, which occurs naturally below the ground, bubbled up through the cracks in the earth. When it evaporated, the sticky asphalt would be left behind. The asphalt preserved the bones of the trapped animals.

No dinosaurs were ever found here. They had disappeared some 65 million years earlier. The fossil treasure began to be discovered just over 100 years ago as the asphalt was mined. Scientists have now discovered millions of fossils here: There are 140 different species of plants and more than 420 species of animals. Many are species that are now

{ What's Cool? Posing as a motorcycle cop at the Discovery Center at the Petersen Automotive Museum.

extinct, like the powerful dire wolf. More than 3,600 have been recovered here, more than any other species of mammal. Scientists think so many perished here because they may have hunted in packs.

Inside the **Page Museum at the La Brea Tar Pits** (5801 Wilshire Blvd., Los Angeles; 323-934-7243; tarpits.org) at the site, you can see an exhibit of more than 400 dire wolf skulls. See how the animals must have felt as you try to pull out weighted handles that have been stuck in tar.

You'll also learn about the "La Brea Woman," the only human skeleton that has been found here.

DID YOU KNOW?

During the holidays, there is "snow" every night at The Grove Shopping Plaza (189 The Grove Dr., Los Angeles; 323-900-8080; thegrovela.com).

And during the week, if you're lucky, you can watch scientists working behind a wall, cleaning and identifying more fossils. You can also walk around the area and see some of the pits yourself—even how some of the fossils look as they're uncovered.

Many kids think the La Brea Tar Pits is Los Angeles's best museum. But remember that this is a city full of museums with kid-appeal. In fact, this area of LA is called Museum Row because it is home to La Brea Tar Pits, the Petersen Automotive Museum, and—right next door to the tar pits—the Los Angeles County Museum of Art, which is the largest art museum in the western part of the country. Ask about the classes for kids. And check out the Boone Children's Gallery.

Art or cars? At the **Petersen Automotive Museum** (6060 Wilshire Blvd., Los Angeles; 323-930-CARS; petersen.org), you can race your brother in a Hot Wheels car. Wow! There are so many different kinds of cars—trucks, buses, limos, SUVs, Model Ts, and plenty of two-wheeled motorcycles, scooters, and minibikes, too. Make sure to check out the Discovery Center that's just for kids.

Got plenty of time? You're going to need it to explore the **LA County Museum of Art** (5905 Wilshire Blvd., Los Angeles; 323-857-6000; lacma.org). It's the biggest art museum in the entire western US. Its collections span the entire history of art from ancient pieces to modern works—with pieces from Africa, the US, China, Egypt, and Europe.

What kind of art do you like to make?

{ **What's Cool?** Seeing stars at The Grove Shopping Plaza who are on a break from the nearby CBS Television City.

Farmers Market Are Fun!

At the **Original Farmers Market** (6333 W. 3rd St., Los Angeles; 866-993-9211; farmersmarketla.com) in Los Angeles there are more than 100 shops and restaurants. Restaurants have been part of the mix since 1934. Vacations are a great time to try new foods, and there is no better place than the farmers market, which is also a good place for souvenir hunting.

Look around and try to imagine this place on busy West 3rd Street as a farm. When Arthur Gilmore came west from Illinois in 1870, he became a dairy farmer here at the corner of 3rd and Fairfax in LA.

At the turn of the 20th century, he needed more water for his expanding herd, so he started drilling for water and found oil. Gilmore Oil Company went on to become the primary source of fuel in the West. Fast-forward to the height of the Great Depression: Local promoters asked E. B. Gilmore—Arthur Gilmore's son and now head of the business—if they could invite farmers to sell produce from trucks on the vacant land that once was the dairy farm. That was the beginning of what has become a favorite LA spot for tourists, locals, and celebs.

Saber-Toothed Tigers

They were the size of the modern African lion and most likely lived and hunted in packs. Scientists think they even took care of their old and sick friends and relatives. Saber-toothed cats had powerful front legs and short tails. That means, scientists say, that they would ambush rather than outrun their prey. Today, they have no close living relatives. Bones from nearly 2,000 saber-toothed cats have been found at **La Brea Tar Pits** (5801 Wilshire Blvd., Los Angeles; 323-934-7243; tarpits .org). They're the state fossil of California.

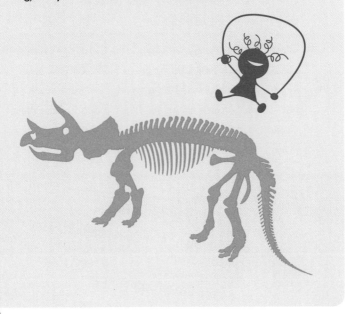

Cowboys & Paintings

- Try your hand gold panning on weekends at **The Autry National Center** in Griffith Park (4700 Western Heritage Way, Los Angeles; 323-667-2000; theautry.org). At this museum, you can find out everything you ever wanted to know about cowboys and cowgirls—real ones and the ones in movies.

- If you want to see what's really new on the art scene, head to the **Museum of Contemporary Art** (250 S. Grand Ave., Los Angeles; 213-626-6222; moca.org). It focuses on all kinds of modern art—even some types of performance art that allow you to participate.

- Check out the zigzag pathway at the **Central Garden of the Getty Center Los Angeles** (1200 Getty Center Dr., Los Angeles; 310-440-7300; getty.edu) where you will also find art and activity kits in the Pop-Up Shop of the West Pavilion, and at the Getty Villa Malibu (17985 Pacific Coast Hwy., Pacific Palisades), visit the Family Forum and the Outer

DID YOU KNOW?

You can see downtown LA, the Santa Monica Mountains, and the Pacific Ocean all from the Getty Center (1200 Getty Center Dr., Los Angeles; 310-440-7300; getty.edu). It's a great place to take a picture of your family!

Peristyle with all the wall paintings of birds, lizards, and other creatures. You'll love the art detective cards at the Getty Center Los Angeles.

- The **Norton Simon Museum of Art** (411 W. Colorado Blvd., Pasadena; 626-449-6840; nortonsimon.org) in Pasadena covers seven centuries of European art. Stop in the sculpture garden.

- See the paintings of children at the **Huntington Library** (1151 Oxford Rd., San Marino; 626-405-2100; huntington .org). You'll find art collections and botanical gardens (see if you can find Thomas Gainsborough's famous *Blue Boy*). The Huntington also has wonderful gardens perfect for cartwheels (look for the koi fish and frogs in the ponds) and even a Japanese House.

- **The Pacific Asia Museum** (46 N. Los Robles Ave., Pasadena; 626-449-2742; pacificasiamuseum.org), meanwhile, is the place to go to learn more about China and Japan.

TELL THE ADULTS:

Arts for the Next Generation: LACMA is the nation's only free youth membership program! NexGen offers free general admission to anyone 17 and under as well as one accompanying adult. To join, visit the LACMA box office or print the enrollment form and mail it in. Visiting a large art museum can sometimes be overwhelming for families. Here are some suggestions from the LA County Museum of Art (5905 Wilshire Blvd., Los Angeles; 323-857-6000; lacma.org) to up the fun:

A LOCAL KID SAYS:
"A good museum to go to is the Getty if you like art. It's enormous!"
—Chloe, 11

- Start with, "What do you see?" Let each person share what is going on.

- Have a seat—sit on the floor! (Just don't block any doorways.) Some galleries also have benches.

What's Cool? Being an extra on a movie set. Check out beinamovie.com.

- Let the kids decide what to see.

- The modern art galleries on the 2nd floor of the Ahmanson Building are spacious, playful, and fun for families. Also try traveling the globe by visiting art from all over the world!

- Don't try to see everything! Twenty minutes to one hour is plenty of time in the galleries.

- Burn off some energy in LACMA's sculpture gardens.

- Visit the Boone Children's Gallery where the kids can paint, read, or just hang out.

- Make art and go on a tour at Andell Family Sundays—nearly every Sunday 12:30 to 3:30 p.m.

DID YOU KNOW?

The LA County Museum of Art isn't just one building. It is a big campus with seven buildings spread out on 20 acres in the heart of Los Angeles.

Learning Tolerance

Do you know people who hate other people just because of how they look or the religion that they practice? Do you know what "prejudiced" means?

For older kids—and their parents—the **Museum of Tolerance** (9786 W. Pico Blvd., Los Angeles; 310-553-8403; museumoftolerance.com) is a terrific place to learn about prejudice and how it hurts people. You'll understand what led to the civil rights movement and contemporary issues like hate crimes on the Internet. See places in the world where human rights violations are ongoing. You'll learn about the Holocaust in which 1.5 million Jewish children were murdered, along with their families. The Museum of Tolerance isn't a fun place, but it's one you'll be glad you visited. The exhibits will make you think about lots of things. For example, what do you do when you see a gang of kids being mean to someone on the playground?

A LOCAL KID SAYS:
"My sister and I love the Noah's Ark exhibit at the Skirball Cultural Center. I like all the different art there."
—Olivia, 10

LA WORD SEARCH

Billboards
Fun
La Brea Tar Pits
Saber Tooth
Sunset

Fossils
Getty Center
Pacific Ocean
Santa Monica
The Grove

```
S  W  L  D  R  P  X  W  F  U  N  F  V
A  U  A  B  V  A  S  U  N  S  E  T  O
B  M  B  M  R  C  O  A  R  E  G  A  A
E  T  R  R  B  I  E  B  I  L  E  R  L
R  P  E  C  I  F  A  C  M  A  T  A  N
T  S  A  N  L  I  F  Q  R  R  T  T  F
O  I  T  Q  L  C  R  I  V  P  Y  H  O
O  D  A  Z  B  O  N  O  M  N  C  E  S
T  N  R  Y  O  C  C  J  A  R  E  G  S
H  L  P  M  A  E  K  O  S  M  N  R  I
Y  F  I  O  R  A  H  L  R  E  T  O  L
J  U  T  R  D  N  Q  X  T  K  E  V  S
E  C  S  M  S  N  R  S  E  W  R  E  N
S  A  N  T  A  M  O  N  I  C  A  B  C
```

See page 152 for the answer key.

4

Lights! Camera! Action!

Hollywood & Universal Studios

The future of the human race is counting on you!

That's how it will feel anyway on Transformers: The Ride-3D at **Universal Studios Hollywood** (100 Universal City Plaza, Universal City; 1-800-UNIVERSAL; universal studioshollywood.com). Yes, it's based on the popular movies and gives you the chance to fight alongside Optimus Prime and protect  the AllSpark from Decepticons more than 4 stories tall. Cool! You can find out more at prepareforbattle.com.

You'll find plenty at Universal Studios to amuse, entertain, and yes, scare you. Head to the House of Horrors and your worst nightmares will come true before your eyes as you wind through a maze of fright and come face-to-face with characters such as Frankenstein, the Wolf Man, and Chucky. This ride is not recommended for scaredy-cats!

{ **What's Cool?** Walking around the VIP Lounge where celebrities meet at the Dolby Theatre (6801 Hollywood Blvd., Los Angeles; 323-308-6300; dolbytheatre.com) on the night of the Academy Awards. You can do that when you take a tour.

Ever watch the *Simpsons* and wish you could join Homer, Marge, Bart, Lisa, and Maggie on a family trip to Krustyland, the theme park created by Krusty the Clown? Now you can on Universal Studios Hollywood's Simpsons Ride. Once you board your vehicle, hold on tight as you embark on a ride flying, floating, and crashing through Krustyland.

Take the **Hollywood Studio Tour.** It will show you the most famous movie back lot in the world. Many movies have been filmed here, including portions of *War of the Worlds, Back to the Future,* and *How the Grinch Stole Christmas.* Watch out—you'll get all shook up in the middle of an earthquake, barely escape a great white shark, and just make it over a collapsing bridge at the last second. You'll be shaken and flooded and spinned. Ready to meet King Kong?

When you've had enough excitement, go goof around with *Curious George,* get soaked in a

500-gallon water dump, and play catch with thousands of flying foam balls. Ride a raft through Jurassic Park and escape a velociraptor and a *Tyrannosaurus rex*. You might meet famous characters like Shrek, Scooby-Doo, and SpongeBob SquarePants.

You're guaranteed to laugh at the Animal Actors Stage as you watch Hollywood's top animal trainers work with animal stars. Shrek 4-D will put you right in the middle of the action. Feel the water, wind, and mist?

Make sure you've got your autograph book too—in case you bump into Shrek, Donkey, Princess Fiona, SpongeBob SquarePants, Optimus Prime, and other characters in the park.

Do you like scary coasters? You'll love Revenge of the Mummy The Ride.

If you're lucky, you might catch a glimpse of some show or movie being filmed. Even better, you might see a movie star. They work here every day.

DID YOU KNOW?

Universal Studios Hollywood is more than a theme park. It's a working studio for TV shows and movies and has been around for nearly 100 years.

It's hard to believe people have been making movies in Hollywood since before your great-grandparents were born. And ever since the beginning, thou-

sands have been following their dreams here—many traveling to the area when they were just teenagers. A few really have been "discovered" in drugstores or on the beach. But more end up waiting tables or working behind the cameras. Talk to your waiter or waitress at dinner. Chances are he or she is a would-be actor/comedian/singer.

You can walk the **Hollywood Walk of Fame** (323-469-8311; hollywoodchamber.net)—along Hollywood Boulevard from Gower Street to Sycamore Avenue and along Vine Street from Yucca to Sunset Boulevard. You'll see all of the brass stars with celebrities' names. Even Mickey Mouse and Snow White have

stars. It's one of Hollywood's biggest attractions. See if you can find imprints of the magic wands of *Harry Potter* stars Daniel Radcliffe and Emma Watson or *Star Wars* robot R2D2's tread marks. You'll find Mickey Mouse at 6925 Hollywood Blvd. and Bugs Bunny at 7007 Hollywood Blvd. Stop in front of **TCL Chinese Theatre,** formally known as Grauman's Chinese Theatre (6925 Hollywood Blvd., Los Angeles; 323-465-4847; tclchinesetheatres.com), on Hollywood Boulevard, to see footprints and handprints that many stars have made in the cement over the years.

By 1922, 52 different studios were located in the LA area. And the town that began as just one house in a fig orchard grew first into a neighborhood named Hollywoodland and then into a bustling city—the capital of entertainment.

Universal Studios offered tours almost from the start. Tourists paid a quarter, and the studio gave them lunch. They could cheer or boo as much as they wanted. Movies had no sound then. The words of actors and actresses were written across the screen. But once sound pictures began to be produced, those early tours ended. Universal Studios didn't reopen to visitors for more than 30 years. And when it did, there wasn't much to see—just a makeup demonstration, a performance by stuntmen, and some costumes.

Now Universal Studios is one of California's top attractions, even more so now that **Universal CityWalk** (100 Universal City Plaza, Universal City; 818-622-4455; citywalkhollywood.com) is open on the hill just above the studios. Check out the 27 different facades of California architecture! Besides the restaurants and movie theaters, there are shops that sell everything from LA Raiders sweatshirts to movie memorabilia to windup toys.

CityWalk is a great place to hang out. There are no cars—just people of all ages. If you're planning to eat here, you can taste everything from sushi to burgers to a meal that comes with a mariachi performance. But come early: The place is jam-packed, particularly on weekend nights and during the summer. It's how you wish all city blocks were—safe, cool, and most of all, fun.

What souvenir are you going to buy?

Watching the Action

If you're 12—most shows require you to be at least that old—you can become part of a studio audience for your favorite show. Most shows are taped from August through March. You can order tickets online.

- Audiences Unlimited, Inc. (818-260-0041; tvtickets.com)

- Paramount Pictures Studio Tour (5555 Melrose Ave., Melrose Gate Visitor Entrance, Hollywood; 323-956-1777; paramountstudiotour.com)

- Universal Studios Hollywood (100 Universal City Plaza, Universal City; 1-800-UNIVERSAL; universalstudioshollywood .com/attractions/studio-tour). You might also be able to get free tickets at Universal's theme park.

A LOCAL KID SAYS:
"My favorite attraction at Universal Studios is Jurassic Park The Ride!"
—Wyatt, 12

- CBS Television City (7800 Beverly Blvd., Los Angeles; 323-575-2345; cbstelevisioncity.com/tickets). You can pick up free tickets for live tapings at the ticket window, on the west side of CBS TV City. For tickets by mail to CBS shows, send a self-addressed stamped envelope to CBS Tickets, 7800 Beverly Blvd., Los Angeles, CA 90036. Specify the show you want to see, the preferred date, and the number of people who wish to attend.

- More information for how to request tickets to NBC shows, including *The Voice* and *America's Got Talent,* can be found on the website at nbc.com/tickets.

DID YOU KNOW?

There's a 19-screen movie theater, IMAX, iFly Hollywood's indoor skydiving, restaurants, shops, and more all at Universal CityWalk.

{ What's Cool? The Special Effects Stage at Universal Studios Hollywood, where you can learn the secrets behind movie magic.

51

TELL THE ADULTS

- If you are planning to hit Southern California's top attractions like Universal Studios, SeaWorld, Disneyland, and Disney California Adventure, consider the Southern California CityPASS, which will save you big bucks. You can also buy the CityPASS online or at any CityPASS attraction for the same price (citypass.com/southern-california).

- Most of the attractions at Universal Studios Hollywood are meant for grade-schoolers and older. (One attraction younger kids will love is the Adventures of Curious George.) You can de-stress the experience by signing on for The VIP Experience, which gives you exclusive back lot access, a gourmet lunch, and a personal theme park guide who will get you the best seats at all the shows and help you cut all of the lines. Such pampering doesn't come cheap ($299 per person), but it may be worth it if your time is limited and you want to feel like a celebrity.

> **DID YOU KNOW?**
>
> More than 100 animals—everything from dogs to pigs to birds—perform at Universal Studios Hollywood.

- If what you really want is to cut the lines at Universal Studios Hollywood, you can get a Front of Line Pass (prices start at $129) that includes the park admission and onetime priority access to each ride and show.

- There are plenty of restaurant choices in the park as well as outside at Universal CityWalk.

- And if you know ahead of time when you plan to visit Universal Studios, you can save money by buying your tickets online.

- Once you get there, make sure to get in line for the shows early. Once they start, you can't get seated, and you don't want to miss the special effects.

DID YOU KNOW?

The Hollywood Museum (1660 N. Highland Ave., Hollywood; 323-464-7776; thehollywoodmuseum.com) inside the Max Factor Building has more showbiz treasures—everything from costumes to props to scripts, even stars' cars—than anywhere in the world.

Scary Rides

Are you ready?

Universal Studios Hollywood (100 Universal City Plaza, Universal City; 1-800-UNIVERSAL; universalstudioshollywood .com) is especially known for its thrilling and fast attractions like Revenge of the Mummy The Ride and Transformers: The Ride-3D.

First, you have to see if you are tall enough. No tiptoes either!

Next, don't make yourself do something you are scared about. That's no fun! Every ride typically has a way to "escape" if you change your mind when you are standing in line.

These rides can be very dark, bumpy, and loud. If you get motion sickness like a lot of kids and grown-ups, you probably want to skip rides that have a lot of sharp curves. Take a virtual tour of the parks beforehand to see what rides you might want to skip this time. There are plenty of other fun attractions!

Remember, a visit to a theme park is supposed to be fun. You don't have to ride any attraction you don't want to! And there's always next time.

A LOCAL KID SAYS:
"Universal Studios is my favorite thing to do in LA."
—Rafael, 12

The HOLLYWOOD Sign

Look up into the Hollywood hills. You can't miss it—the letters are the size of a 5-story building. It spells out HOLLY-WOOD and has been a landmark since 1923. The idea was to advertise a subdivision called Hollywoodland. Each letter was 50 feet high and 30 feet wide. They were constructed with telegraph poles hauled up the mountain by mules. Four thousand lightbulbs ensured that the sign would be seen at night. Eventually, the letters L, A, N, and D slid down the mountain. The lightbulbs were stolen. By the end of 1979, a brand-new HOLLYWOOD sign—this time without lights—replaced the first one. It cost $249,000—nearly 12 times the original. You can pose for a picture with the sign in the background at the entrance arch of the Hollywood & Highland shopping and entertainment complex (6801 Hollywood Blvd., Hollywood; 323-817-0200; hollywoodandhighland.com).

Using the key at the bottom, write the letters under the symbols to figure out the secret phrase.

For example:  = b i r d

_ _ _ _ _ _ _ _ _   _ _ _ _

_ _   _ _ _ _

a = ✔   b = 🚲   c = 🏙   d = ✈   e = 🎁

f = 🏭   g = 🏛   h = 🏠   i = 〰   j = 🏘

k = ✿   l = ?   m = ❗   n = 👁   o = ⛵

p = 🛤   q = ⛺   r = 🚉   s = ✦   t = 🌉

u = 📢   v = ◈   w = 🚩   x = 🔊   y = ♥

z = 💐   . = ◨   ! = 🚌   , = 🌶

See page 152 for the answer key.

Now try and make your own secret messages in the space below.

{ What's Cool? Posing with a "movie star," favorite character, or celeb (maybe Justin Bieber?) carved in wax at Madame Tussaud's on Hollywood Boulevard (6933 Hollywood Blvd., Hollywood, CA, 90028; 323-798-1670; madametussauds.com/Hollywood).

5
Stars, Koalas
& Cowboys

Ready to play?

Local kids like to go to **Griffith Park** (4730 Crystal Springs Dr., Los Angeles; 323-913-4688; laparks.org/dos/parks/griffithpk). With more than 4,200 acres, there's plenty of room to hike, ride horses, swim, play tennis or golf, or just goof around. It's the biggest city-run park in the country—with more than 50 miles of hiking trails. The **Griffith Observatory** (2800 E. Observatory Ave., Los Angeles; 213-473-0800; griffithobs.org) and **The Autry National Center** (4700 Western Heritage Way, Los Angeles; 323-667-2000; theautry.org) are also in the park. Gene Autry was a famous singing cowboy in movies and TV, and the Autry Center is where you will find out everything about cowboys—real and in the movies. You can even see the original Lone Ranger's mask.

DID YOU KNOW?

Walt Disney got the idea for Disneyland when he brought his daughters to Griffith Park and watched them ride the merry-go-round. He imagined a place where parents and kids could have fun together.

The park has an old-fashioned merry-go-round, pony rides, and a miniature train. Like trains? Stop at **Travel Town** (5200 Zoo Dr., Los Angeles; 323-662-5874; traveltown.org), an outdoor vehicle museum known for its locomotives and miniature train rides. During the Christmas season, you can board the Santa Express and take a ride through all the holiday lights. You can meet Santa, too!

Whenever you come, bring a picnic and spend the whole day.

If you'd rather watch animals than people, you won't want to miss the **Los Angeles Zoo and Botanical Gardens** (5333 Zoo Dr., Los Angeles; 323-644-4200; lazoo.org) when you visit Griffith Park. Check out the zoo website before you visit to learn more about the animals and play online games (click on "fun zone").

A VISITING KID SAYS:
"My favorite thing to do in LA was to go hiking in Griffith Park."
—Douglas, 14, Westport, CT

You'll find more than 1,100 animals here—from kangaroos to hippopotamuses to orangutans to ostriches. Don't miss the Elephants of Asia, a habitat for endangered Asian elephants. Come to the Elephants of Asia habitat at 11:00 a.m. and see how the animal keepers train the giant elephants! (They can eat 330 pounds of food every day!) Move from one viewing area to another— you'll see different things—like how the elephants take baths. At the Campo Gorilla Reserve you'll laugh as the gorillas play. Have you ever seen a poison dart frog or a Fiji Island iguana? They're really cool looking! You can see them and more at the zoo's LAIR exhibit, which stands for Living Amphibians, Invertebrates, and Reptiles. Here's your chance to walk through a crocodile swamp! See if you can hear the animals "talk."

{ **What's Cool?** Feeding a rhino on a special Indian Rhino Encounter Tour at the Los Angeles Zoo and Botanical Gardens (lazoo.org/visit/showsandactivities).

Ready to meet some goats? These are Nigerian dwarf goats that only grow to be 2 feet tall and, at most, 50 pounds. Smaller maybe than your dog! You'll find them at Muriel's Ranch at the Winnick Family Children's Zoo, where you can pet the goats and the sheep.

If you like carousels, you'll love the Conservation Carousel with its hand-carved animals and the Neil Papiano Play Park with its animal-themed climbing sculptures. If you're hot, this is a good place to cool off in the water misters.

What's the weirdest animal you saw at the zoo?

A LOCAL KID SAYS:
"My favorite museum is the Griffith Observatory because it's interesting to see all of the displays about astronomy."
—Kimberly, 15

Endangered Species and How You Can Help

The Los Angeles Zoo and Botanical Gardens is home to 1,100 animals, many of which are rare or endangered. An endangered species is an animal or plant that is in danger of disappearing completely from our planet.

At the LAIR exhibit—that stands for Living Amphibians, Invertebrates, and Reptiles—you can meet animals that were taken from international smugglers and placed in the care of the zoo—Komodo dragons, Chinese alligators, and maybe the world's rarest tortoise. You can help save endangered species when you adopt an animal at the Los Angeles Zoo and Botanical Gardens. Choose an animal and for a small donation you will be the guardian of that species at the zoo for a year (lazoo.org/support/adopt).

Many other species are threatened, which means that unless conservation efforts are started, they're likely to become endangered. Animals and humans are part of one world with one ocean, and it is up to us to protect it. Every day, you can do small, simple things to help the planet:

- Turn off lights when you leave a room.

DID YOU KNOW?

California is home to the highest peak in the continental US (Mount Whitney) and the lowest valley (Death Valley). That means there are a lot of different kinds of native plants. You can see them at the Los Angeles Zoo and Botanical Gardens in Griffith Park.

- Turn off the television if no one is watching it.

- Create a recycling center in your home and recycle newspapers, glass, and aluminum cans.

- Turn off the water while brushing your teeth.

- Use both sides of a piece of paper.

- Plant wildflowers in your garden instead of picking them from nature.

- Reduce the amount of trash you create: Reuse your lunch bag each day.

- Don't buy animals or plants taken illegally from the wild or that are native to your area. Ask where they're from.

- Share what you know with family and friends.

Play Ball!

Basketball, baseball, soccer, hockey … whatever sport is your passion (except pro football), you can watch it in LA:

- The **Los Angeles Galaxy** plays major league soccer at its highest level. (18400 S. Avalon Blvd., Carson; 310-630-2200; lagalaxy.com)

- The **Los Angeles Dodgers'** stadium is really cool! (1000 Elysian Park Ave., Los Angeles; 866-363-4377; losangeles .dodgers.mlb.com)

> ### DID YOU KNOW?
>
> LA Lakers basketball legend Magic Johnson is now one of the owners of the Los Angeles Dodgers.
>
> UCLA has more NCAA team championships than any other university.

- The **Los Angeles Angels** used to be called the California Angels and also the Anaheim Angels. (2000 E. Gene Autry Way, Anaheim; 714-940-2000; losangeles.angels.mlb.com)

- The **Anaheim Ducks** are in the National Hockey League and play at the Honda Center. (2695 E. Katella Ave., Anaheim; 714-704-2408; ducks.nhl.com)

- The **Staples Center** (1111 S. Figueroa St., Los Angeles; 213-742-7340; staplescenter.com) is home to a number of teams, including:

The **Los Angeles Lakers**. You might see your favorite celebrities watching courtside at a Lakers game. (nba.com/lakers)

The **Los Angeles Clippers** of the NBA (nba.com/clippers)

The **Los Angeles Sparks** of the WNBA (wnba.com/sparks)

The **Los Angeles Kings** of the National Hockey League (kings.nhl.com)

You can also watch plenty of men and women's college action in just about every sport—sand volleyball, basketball, golf, tennis, track and field, swimming, and water polo from the USC Trojans (3501 Watt Way, Los Angeles; 213-740-3843; usctrojans.com) to the UCLA Bruins (405 Hilgard Ave., Los Angeles; 310-825-4321; uclabruins.com). Check the websites to see what sports events might be going on when you visit.

A LOCAL KID SAYS:
"I like the LA Dodgers because living so close to their stadium has given me a community that loves baseball; it's a family thing."
—Guadalupe, 15

TELL THE ADULTS

Griffith Park (4730 Crystal Springs Dr., Los Angeles; 323-913-4688; laparks.org/dos/parks/griffithpk) has a 53-mile network of hiking trails, fire roads, and bridle paths. One of the best hikes in the park is from the **Griffith Observatory** (2800 E. Observatory Ave., Los Angeles; 213-473-0800; griffithobs.org) parking lot to the summit of Mount Hollywood, the highest peak of the park. The views are great! But remember, this is a wilderness area with some wild quail, foxes, and other animals.

For even more hiking, head to the **Will Rogers State Historic Park** (1501 Will Rogers State Park Rd., Pacific Palisades; 310-454-8212; parks.ca.gov) in Pacific Palisades, just inland from the ocean between Santa Monica and Malibu. You might be able to watch a polo match here. At the very least, there's lots of space to run and jump. Ask about the nature walks for families.

DID YOU KNOW?

The HOLLYWOOD sign is in Griffith Park.

Griffith Park is five times the size of New York's Central Park and one of the largest urban green spaces in the entire country.

And whenever you are hiking with kids:

- Make sure you have a plan in place in case someone gets separated from the group. Tell the kids to "hug a tree" and stay where they are until you return for them. Make sure they have your cell phone number and where you are staying written on a card in their pocket. They may not remember!

- Have reusable water bottles and healthy snacks in everyone's backpack.

- Use sunscreen, even if it is cloudy.

- Stash rain gear in the packs.

- Remember it is about the journey! If everyone gets tired or the hike is too difficult, just turn back.

- Don't forget the snacks. They come in handy when the going gets rough—or as a reward at the end of the hike.

Star Lingo

We're not talking about movie stars now. We're talking about the language that astronomers use at the Griffith Observatory, one of southern California's most popular attractions (2800 E. Observatory Ave., Los Angeles; 213-473-0800; griffithobs.org).

- **Astronomy** is the study of space.

- The **atom** is the simplest building block of the universe.

- A **comet** is a small icy object from the outer part of the solar system.

- An **extraterrestrial** is any object, living or not, that originates from some place other than earth.

- An **extremophile** is an organism that has adapted to survive in extreme environments.

- A **galaxy** is a massive collection of stars and celestial objects bound together into a single system by gravity.

- Earth and our sun and planets are all part of the **Milky Way galaxy.**

- A **solar system** is a group of planets, moons, asteroids, comets, and other small objects that orbit one star.

- The **sun** is the only star in our solar system.

SPORTS WORD SCRAMBLE

Can you unscramble these LA-area sports teams and then write in what sport each team plays?

Team Name		**Sport**
GELSAN	_____	_____
PERSCLIP	_____	_____
GERSDOD	_____	_____
CKSDU	_____	_____
XYGALA	_____	_____
INGKS	_____	_____
SARKLE	_____	_____
PARSKS	_____	_____

See page 152 for the answer key.

6

Tacos, Sushi
& Souvenirs

Melrose Avenue (melrose avenue-shop.com) might not be the place your mom and dad would go to people-watch.

But you'll love it. It's funky—and weird and fun. The busiest stretch is between Fairfax and La Brea Avenues.

People come here to shop and to be seen. Everyone is looking to see what's hot—and what's not. There are many one-of-a-kind boutiques where you can buy everything from leather vests to jeans to Halloween masks. You'll find hats and plastic bracelets.

DID YOU KNOW?

Vietnam's national dish is pho—white rice noodles in a clear broth and topped with sliced meat. The signature Korean dish you should try is beef ribs (kalbi) that are grilled right at your table!

What's Cool? Sightseeing in shorts and flip-flops—in the wintertime!

Local kids say this is the place to see the new styles before anyone even recognizes that they're in fashion. If you see cool young people wearing a new style on TV, it probably began here on Melrose Avenue!

Of course you've got to check out **Rodeo Drive** (between Wilshire and Santa Monica Boulevards; 310-308-8333; rodeodrive-bh.com/index4.html) in Beverly Hills, too—even if you can't afford anything here, it's fun to walk around. Go a block over to

A LOCAL KID SAYS:
"Visiting kids should not leave without a sweater that says 'California.' They're very popular now."
—Chris, 14

Beverly Drive for less expensive stores where you can actually shop, not just gawk.

Los Angeles is a great place for shopping—and eating! Make it a goal to try something you've never eaten before. Have you ever had a fresh tamale? Chinese dim sum?

And shop for things you can't find at home or at least

in a shopping mall that is different than at home. You can take your pick of shopping centers, whatever you want to buy:

- Westfield Century City (10250 Santa Monica Blvd., Los Angeles; 310-277-3898; westfield.com/centurycity) has more than 100 stores, restaurants, and even a dog park.

- For a Chinese parasol, go to Chinatown Galleries in downtown LA's Chinatown (North Broadway at North Hill Street, Downtown, Los Angeles; 213-680-0243; chinatownla.com). You will find plenty of T-shirts, too.

A VISITING KID SAYS:
"Save up for souvenirs before you come!"
—Lexie, 10, El Paso, TX

- For leather sandals and woven blankets, check out Olvera Street in the oldest part of downtown LA, which has stalls selling everything from woven blankets to candles (between Cesar Chavez Avenue and Arcadia Street; 213-687-4391; calleolvera.com).

- For anything Ferrari (as well as everything else you might want) go to the Beverly Center (8500 Beverly Blvd., Los Angeles; 310-854-0070; beverlycenter.com).

- For Hollywood souvenirs, walk all along Hollywood Boulevard near the Dolby Theatre (6801 Hollywood Blvd., Los Angeles). There's also the Hollywood & Highland Center (6801 Hollywood Blvd., Los Angeles; 323-308-6300; hollywoodandhighland.com).

- For surfer clothes, the Third Street Promenade in Santa Monica (3rd Street between Broadway and Wilshire Boulevard close to the ocean; 310-393-8355; downtownsm.com) has everything you could possibly need.

- For shopping like royalty, there is the Citadel Outlets within a building that was constructed to look like a castle (100 Citadel Dr., Los Angeles; 323-888-1724; citadeloutlets.com).

- For shopping where movie stars' kids go: The Grove is where you can take a trolley from one end to another and find American Girl Place, Pottery Barn Kids, and Quicksilver Youth, among other stores (189 The Grove Dr., Los Angeles; 323-900-8080; thegrovela.com).

What's your shopping style?

What's Cool? Trying some kind of food you've never had before. Check online at findlafoodtrucks.com to see where the famous LA food trucks are, whether you want a grilled cheese, Chinese dumplings, or tacos.

Music for All Ears

Whatever music you like, you'll find it in LA where so many musicians live and work:

- **The Hollywood Bowl** (in a natural bowl in the Hollywood hills!) is one of the largest outdoor amphitheaters anywhere (2301 N. Highland Ave., Hollywood; 323-850-2000; hollywoodbowl.com).

- **The Greek Theatre** in Griffith Park is outside (2700 N. Vermont Ave., Los Angeles; 323-665-5857; greektheatrela.com).

- **The Walt Disney Concert Hall** (hear the Los Angeles Master Chorale, the resident chorus) is home to the Los Angeles Philharmonic orchestra and has special kids' events in the outdoor amphitheater (111 S. Grand Ave., Los Angeles; 323-850-2000; laphil.com/philpedia/about-walt-disney-concert-hall).

- **Dolby Theatre,** besides being home to the Academy Awards, is also home to a Cirque du Soleil show (6801 Hollywood Blvd., Los Angeles; 323-466-1428; cirquedusoleil.com).

Eating Smart on Vacation

Vacations are a good time to try different foods than just what is on a kids' menu. That's especially true in Los Angeles where you'll find restaurants that feature food from all around the world as well as vegetables and meats from local farmers. Here's how you can eat healthier and try new foods:

- If there is something you like on the grown-up menu, ask if you can get a half portion or order an appetizer size.

- Choose fruit as a snack instead of chips or candy.

- Visit and talk to the farmers at The Original Farmers Market (6333 W. 3rd St., Los Angeles; 866-993-9211; farmersmarketla .com) or Grand Central Market (317 S. Broadway, Los Angeles; 213-624-2378; grandcentralsquare.com) to see what's grown in Southern California (everything from mangoes to peppers), and you can try all varieties of food.

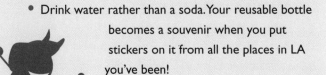

- Drink water rather than a soda. Your reusable bottle becomes a souvenir when you put stickers on it from all the places in LA you've been!

SOUVENIR SMARTS

Mickey Mouse ears ...a Lakers cap ...a Simpsons or Trans-formers T-shirt at Universal Studios Hollywood—whatever you don't want to leave Los Angeles without, you are bound to find it here. Let's not forget there are many shopping malls (discoverlosangeles.com can tell you exactly where they are)!

But shop smart! That means talk to your parents about exactly how much you may spend. Save your allowance and birthday money before you come. Some families save loose change in a jar to use for souvenirs.

Do you want to use your money for one big souvenir (a stuffed Mickey or a pricey sweatshirt)? Or several smaller ones? Do you want a special T-shirt from a particular attrac-tion or with your favorite character on it?

Resist those impulse buys. Wait until the end of the day or the end of the trip to shop. After a few days, you'll get a better idea of what you really can't leave without!

Think about choosing something you could only get in Los Angeles. Start a collection! Collect pins or patches to put on your backpack. What else could you collect?

Fish Tacos!

You've got to eat tacos while you are here. Taco trucks are all over LA, so keep your eyes peeled and see if you can spot one! Those who work at the *Los Angeles Times* say you should go to **Ye Olde Taco House #1**, a stand at 340 S. Hill St. (213-625-2700) just next to Grand Central Market in downtown Los Angeles. Locals really love fish tacos. Try **Señor Fish** (senorfish.net) with several locations or the chains that specialize in them: **Wahoos** (wahoos.com), **Rubio's** (rubios.com), or **Baja Fresh** (bajafresh.com).

A LOCAL KID SAYS:
"Kids shouldn't leave LA without trying fish tacos. Lots of recipes come from Mexico because we are on the border."
—Chloe, 11

DID YOU KNOW?

Los Angeles has the largest Mexican-American population of any city in the US. But there are also large populations of Koreans, Vietnamese, and Filipinos outside their home countries. Immigrants from more than 140 countries live here, making LA an especially good place to try ethnic eats.

Great Places to Grab a Family Meal
Fun Eats!

You can get just about any kind of food in Los Angeles! Here are some family favorites to tell your parents about.

- **Chinatown:** A great place for dumplings. (N. Broadway at North Hill Street, Downtown, Los Angeles; 213-680-0243; chinatownla.com)

- **Huckleberry:** Offers Thursday night family dinners. Check out the homemade bread. The menu changes with the seasons. (1014 Wilshire Blvd., Santa Monica; 310-451-2311; huckleberrycafe.com)

- **L.A. Live:** In downtown LA, this is a great place to eat whether you want sushi, Mexican food, or pizza. (800 W. Olympic Blvd., Los Angeles; 866-LIVE-4LA; lalive.com/eat)

- **Little Tokyo:** Has some of the best sushi in LA. (Downtown, Southeast of the Civic Center; bounded by 1st, Los Angeles; 213-293-5822; littletokyola.org)

- **Mel's Drive-In:** Serving everything from breakfast to burgers and shakes. (1660 N. Highland, Hollywood; 323-465-3111; melsdrive-in.com/menu/kids.html)

- **Mendocino Farms:** A great place to get a sandwich, salad, and soup made from what is in season at the farmers' market. (Several locations in LA, including: 175 S. Fairfax Ave., Los Angeles; 323-934-4261; mendocinofarms.com)

- **Miceli's for Pizza:** Singing waiters across the street from Universal Studios. (3655 Cahuenga Blvd. West, Universal City; 323-851-3344; micelisrestaurant.com)

- **Park's BBQ:** In the heart of LA's Korea district, this is a great place to try Korean barbecue. (1145 S. Western Ave., Los Angeles; 323-373-0700; parksbbq.com)

- **Short Order:** Serves burgers, shakes, and salads that are all made from scratch with ingredients from local farmers and ranchers. (6333 W. 3rd St., #110, Los Angeles; 323-761-7970; shortorderla.com)

What's Cool? Sweet! Hollywood (6801 Hollywood Blvd., Hollywood; 323-462-3111), the largest candy store in the world, which takes up a half acre in the heart of Hollywood. Check out the world's largest gumball machine or the lollipop forest.

Ice Cream, You Scream . . .

These places serve up delicious desserts!

- **Proof Bakery** (3156 Glendale Blvd., Los Angeles; 323-664-8633; proofbakeryla.com)

- **Scoops Westside** for weird and crazy ice cream flavors (3400 Overland Ave., Los Angeles; 323-405-7055; scoops westside.com).

- **Short Cake** for everything from brownies to cookies and sandwiches, too (6333 W. 3rd St., Los Angeles; 323-761-7976; shortcakeLA.com).

- **Sprinkles Cupcakes** is a place where you might meet a celebrity when you order! Try the chocolate marshmallow or peanut butter chocolate! (9635 S. Santa Monica Blvd., Beverly Hills; 310-274-8765; sprinkles.com)

- **Sweet Rose Creamery** for homemade ice cream in Santa Monica. Have you ever had an ice-cream slider with ice cream and bacon? (225 26th St., Santa Monica; 310-260-CONE)

TELL THE ADULTS

Touring a city like Los Angeles can be overwhelming. The more the kids are involved in the planning, the better! Here's how:

- The kids can help plan the itinerary by taking a virtual tour of the theme parks and museums you plan to visit. Start at the discoverlosangeles.com and visitcalifornia.com websites and link to the attractions you plan to visit.

- Make sure each child gets to see one of their top theme park attractions each day of your visit. Alternate whose pick is first!

- Cut the itinerary in half—whether you are touring the city or a major museum. With kids, you aren't going to see everything, so don't even try. The theme park, the monuments, and the museum will all be there next time. Focus on what captures the kids' attention—and yours—and leave when everyone has had enough. Make sure there is time for the hotel pool, the beach, or the playground!

- Let the kids help choose restaurants and what's in your cooler.

- Alternate attractions that cost money with free ones—parks, playgrounds, and the hotel pool.

7

Rollerblades,
Whales & Musclemen

Got some in-line skates or a skateboard?

Hop on a bike. Put on those shades. Head outside with the rest of Southern California to bike, blade, and run along the Pacific Coast, watching people—and maybe even gray whales—as you go. There's lots of coast to cover.

Start in Santa Monica. You can bike along a city bike path or the **South Bay Bicycle Trail** (labikepaths.com) that runs for 22 miles. Try out the equipment on **Muscle Beach** (800-544-5319; musclebeach.net) or join a beach volleyball game. There are lots of free courts.

A VISITING KID SAYS:
"It's cool to see the view from the Ferris wheel on the Santa Monica Pier."
—Ned, 16, New York City

What's Cool? The 9-story-high solar-powered Ferris wheel at Pacific Park in Santa Monica (380 Santa Monica Pier, Santa Monica; 310-260-8744; pacpark.com).

On the **Santa Monica Pier** (200 Santa Monica Pier, Santa Monica; 310-458-8901; santamonicapier.org), you'll find an old carousel with handpainted wooden horses, bumper cars, arcade games, a giant Ferris wheel, and a Fun Zone with rides geared for younger kids (though everyone will love the giant slide). Santa Monica, a few miles west of Los Angeles, has plenty of beaches too— complete with paved bike paths alongside the sand.

Lots of people like to fish from the end of the pier.

A short walk from the Santa Monica beach, you'll find the **Third Street Promenade** (1351 Third Street Promenade, #201, Santa Monica; 310-393-8355; downtownsm.com), a 3-block open-air mall with lots of stores. But the street performers at night and on weekends are the most fun—musicians, mimes, acrobats, even bubble blowers and psychics.

Even if you think museums are boring, you'll want to visit the **Getty Villa** (17985 Pacific Coast Hwy., Pacific Palisades; 310-440-7300; getty.edu) just north of Santa Monica in Malibu. It's famous around the world for its collections from ancient Greece and Rome. At the Family Forum, kids can act out a scene from an ancient vase. Do you want to be an athlete or a monster, or paint a vase? Kids like to roam around the gardens, too. Admission is free, but remind your parents you need to get tickets in advance and pick up the special kids' activity guides to the galleries.

DID YOU KNOW?
Venice, California, was modeled after Venice, Italy, compete with canals and floating gondolas when it was first built in 1904.

{ **What's Cool?** Checking out the boardwalk scene at Venice Beach (1800 Ocean Front Walk, Venice; 310-399-2775; venicebeach.com)—especially on the weekend.

There's a sadder thing you might see in Santa Monica—as well as a few miles away in Venice. There are lots of homeless people here. You may see them sleeping on the beach or sitting in the park.

Walk or in-line skate along **Ocean Front Walk** in Venice (venicebeach.com) and you'll see all kinds of colorful people who are that way because they want to be—bikini-clad women on in-line skates, men with huge muscles working out with weights, palm readers, artists, girls with purple hair, acrobats, musicians, and mimes.

Venice started as one man's fantasy to copy Venice, Italy. And when it was first built, it had canals, floating gondolas, and bridges. The gondolas are gone now, though a few small canals and bridges remain.

Today, people are the attraction. Don't forget your shades.

LA Lifeguards

You'll see them winter and summer patrolling the miles and miles of coastline. They tell you where it's safe to swim and warn you if there are dangerous rip currents that will pull you out to sea. Most importantly, they'll come rescue you if you get in trouble.

There are some 700 lifeguards who work in Los Angeles County, from San Pedro north to Malibu. It's a hard job. They watch the beaches and take care of the rescue equipment. They answer questions, make sure people are following the rules of the beach, administer first aid, and, of course, rescue those who need help. The good part is they get to spend every day at the beach!

A LOCAL KID SAYS:
"One of my favorite things to do at the beach is walk around and feel the breeze of the ocean."
—Juan, 14

The LA County Lifeguards (fire.lacounty.gov/Lifeguards/Lifeguards.asp) are the most highly trained lifeguards in the world. You've got to be in good shape to qualify and then pass a tough swimming test and physical exam. Then you must take a training course to learn everything from first aid to ocean rescues. You've got to pass a written test on all you've learned. Here are some things you can do to help lifeguards do their job—and keep yourself safe:

> **DID YOU KNOW?**
> Gray whales can dive as deep as 500 feet and stay under water for 20 minutes.

- Swim in life-guarded areas.

- Ask lifeguards about surf conditions before you go into the water and never dive into areas close to shore if you don't know how deep the water is.

- Don't panic if you get pulled by a rip current. Call for help. Try to swim at an angle toward shore.

- Avoid swimming near storm drain outlets.

A Trip to Santa Barbara

Locals say Santa Barbara (santabarbaraca.com) is what people think all of Southern California is like—crashing surf, wide sandy beaches, palm trees, dozens of cute shops in red-roofed buildings, volleyball courts on the East Beach (some say it's the best beach in California), and a bike path that winds its way along the beach and through the **Andree Clark Bird Refuge** (1400 E. Cabrillo Blvd., Santa Barbara; 805-564-5418; santabarbara .gov). You can see lots of ducks and other waterbirds along the way.

Santa Barbara is about 90 miles up the coast from Los Angeles, and kids love it here. The Pacific Ocean is on one side; the Santa Ynez Mountains are on the other.

The **Channel Islands**—five of them form a national park—are nearby, off the coast in Ventura (1901 Spinnaker Dr., Ventura; 805-658-5730; nps.gov/chis/index

> **DID YOU KNOW?**
>
> You can join a chess game at the International Chess Park in Santa Monica along Ocean Front Walk. There's even a human-size chessboard (santamonica.com/ visitors/what-to-do/attractions/ chess-park).

A LOCAL KID SAYS:
"My favorite thing to do
at the pier is go fishing!"
—Andrew, 14

.htm). Here you can take a boat trip to look for whales and other sea life (maybe even flying fish) or to explore the undeveloped islands.

In Santa Barbara, you can tool around on the funny-looking four-wheeled bikes called pedalinas. They look more like golf carts than bikes! You can rent them nearby.

Everyone loves the little **Santa Barbara Zoo** (500 Ninos Dr., Santa Barbara; 805-962-5339; sbzoo.org). Check out the miniature train ride.

At the **Ty Warner Sea Center on Stearns Wharf** (211 Stearns Wharf, Santa Barbara; 805-962-2526; sbnature.org/twsc/2.html), you can learn about the marine life off the Santa Barbara coast. You'll see a gigantic life-size model of a gray whale skeleton (there's an 80-foot blue whale skeleton) at the **Santa Barbara Museum of Natural History** (2559 Puesta Del Sol, Santa Barbara; 805-682-4711; sbnature.org). Stick your hands in the Touch Tank and feel what some of the sea creatures are like. Have you ever held a starfish? They're not slimy at all. They feel rough, almost like rocks. Rent gear and go fishing!

Skateboard Lingo

At first, they called it "sidewalk surfing"—putting skate wheels on the bottom of wooden boards—and it started in Southern California among surfers. Today kids—and grown-ups—across the country skateboard, but there's probably nowhere that people skateboard more than in Southern California. There are a lot of skate parks in Southern California (find out where at socalskateparks.com) including at Santa Monica and Venice Beach. Some of the language is similar to what you'll hear surfers say. You don't want to be a poser,

A VISITING KID SAYS:
"The Santa Monica Pier is a great place to buy souvenirs."
—Emily, 13, St. Louis

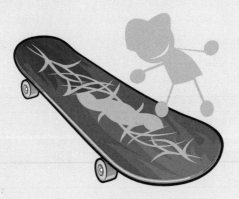

someone who looks like a skater but doesn't really know anything. Here's how to sound like you know what you are talking about at the skate park:

- You are a **skater,** not a skateboarder.

- **Deck** isn't what's in the backyard; it's the wooden part of your skateboard.

- **Sick** means something is really cool. So do ill and gnar (short for gnarly).

- **Sketchy** is something that isn't well done, like a sketchy trick.

- **Bail** is when you either fall or jump off your board before falling.

Fun Can Be Free!

Vacations are expensive. That's why it's great when you find a place that's fun to visit where a lot of things are free—like in and around Santa Monica (santamonica.com). You can:

- Go to the beach! It stretches for 3.5 miles between Venice and Malibu.

- Take a stroll on Santa Monica Pier.

- Take a picnic to the duck pond in Douglas Park (25th Street and Wilshire, Santa Monica; santamonica.patch .com).

- Check out the Santa Monica Pier Aquarium (1600 Ocean Front Walk, Santa Monica; 310-393-6149; healthebay.org/ santa-monica-pier-aquarium) where kids under 12 get in free.

- Cool off at the splash pad in Virginia Avenue Park (May– September).

- Or join a pick-up basketball game (2200 Virginia Ave., Santa Monica; 310-458-8688; smgov.net).

- Watch the trapeze artists at a free show on the Santa Monica Pier.

WHERE IS A FUN PLACE TO VISIT RIGHT ON THE BEACH?

Figure out the missing letters in these destinations and then unscramble them to find the answer. (All of these words can be found in this chapter.)

1.) Dog__own
2.) P__cific Park
3.) Ve__ice
4.) Gray wh__les
5.) __anta Barbara
6.) Cha__nel __slands
7.) __uscle Beach
8.) Andree __lark Bird Refuge
9.) Internati__nal Chess Park
10.) Bird __efuge
11.) Car__interia
12.) L__feguards
13.) St__arns Wharf
14.) J. P__ul Getty Villa

NOW UNSCRAMBLE EACH WORD

_ _ _ _ _   _ _ _ _ _ _   _ _ _ _
5 2 3 1 4   7 9 6 6 8 14   11 12 13 10

See page 153 for the answer key.

8
Surfers, Sand Castles, Lifeguards & Sea Creatures

You'll see them out here even in winter, riding the waves, intent on catching The Big One.

The Los Angeles area is surfer country. Surfers are fun to watch. The beach towns just south of LA are also great spots for building gigantic sand castles, flying kites, browsing for souvenirs, bird watching, or racing along the ocean's edge. There are miles and miles of beach, not to mention carnival games, shops, restaurants, and other assorted sites with kid-appeal, such as the gigantic ship *Queen Mary* (1126 Queens Hwy., Long Beach; 877-342-0738; queen mary.com) moored in Long Beach or the **Cabrillo Marine Aquarium** in San Pedro (3720 Stephen M. White Dr., San Pedro; 310-548-7562; cabrillomarineaquarium.org).

Thousands of families set off on cruises from the **Port of Los Angeles** (425 S. Palos Verdes St., San Pedro; 310-SEA-PORT; portoflosangeles.org) in San Pedro Bay, about 20 miles south of downtown LA. But this port isn't just for passenger ships. There are cargo terminals where everything from cars to clothes to electronics arrives in this country. There's also the **Cabrillo Beach** (3720 Stephen M. White Dr., San Pedro; 310-831-6245; sanpedro.com) where you can swim, fish, or go boat-ing. You can also learn some US history aboard the **USS *Iowa*,** a World War II battleship that now calls the Port of Los Angeles home (250 S. Harbor Blvd., San Pedro;

What's Cool? Making a giant sand creation. Bring along an ice-cream scoop, spatula, ruler, butter knife, spray bottle, gardening trowel, pails, and shovels when you go to the beach. These items and some good ideas are all you need to build a sand sculpture. Here's a tip from experts: Keep the sand really wet. And pack it really hard. Jump up and down on it. It works!

877-446-9261; pacificbattleship
.com). See where the captain was
stationed during battle, the guns,
and the mess deck. During World War II,
there could have been 8,000 meals prepared each day for the crews!

You can take a short cruise to **Santa
Catalina Island** (catalina.com), just a little
more than 20 miles off the coast. In the 1800s, pigeons carried messages between Catalina and the mainland. You
can get there by boat from the beach town of San Pedro
(sanpedro.com) as well as other towns. There's plenty to
explore on the 76-square-mile island. You may even see
bison roaming in the interior. That's because most of the
island is a nature preserve owned
by the Santa Catalina Island
Conservancy (catalina
conservancy.org), formed

A LOCAL KID SAYS:
"I like to go to Leo Carillo Beach
when the tide is out and look
for sea anemones and crabs."
—Cole, 10

{ **What's Cool?** The crawl-in aquarium at the Cabrillo Marine Aquarium
where you are surrounded by ocean life—but never get wet!

to keep the land just the way it is. You'll find hundreds of species of plants, birds, and other animals. There's great snorkeling here, too!

To watch the surfers, head to **Huntington Beach** (ci.huntington-beach.ca.us), where there are more than 8 miles of public beach. You can learn some surfing history and see some of the 20-foot-long boards surfers used in the old days at the **International Surfing Museum** (411 Olive Ave., Huntington Beach; 714-960-3483; surfing museum.org).

Take a walk out on the **Huntington Beach Pier** (huntingtonbeachca.gov)—the original was built in 1914—and watch the action. Some locals say that right off Huntington Pier is the best surfing spot in Orange County. Besides surfing, a lot of people head to the beach here to play volleyball, ride bikes, in-line skate, or just hang out. At Huntington Central Park, there's an

Adventure Playground (huntington beachca.gov), complete with mud slide and a rope bridge. Be prepared to get dirty!

Like birds? You might want to head to the **Bolsa Chica Ecological Conservancy** (3842 Warner Ave., Huntington Beach; 714-846-1114; bolsa chica.org) where you can see all kinds of birds that like the wetlands.

Newport Beach is just a few miles south. Kids especially like the **Balboa Fun Zone** (600 East Bay Ave., Balboa; thebalboa funzone.com). You can ride the famous Ferris wheel or head for the arcade games, the beach, or take a bike ride. There are miles of bike paths! Newport is also a good place to watch the boats—there are thousands moored here. Many people like to take the car ferry across to Balboa Island—it takes just a couple of minutes. You'll almost always find people fishing along Balboa Pier. Try a Balboa Bar—a frozen banana.

DID YOU KNOW?

When waves were flat, surfers tried sidewalk surfing, which became skateboarding. Surfing was also the inspiration for snowboarding.

Fish Friends

Just a few steps from the ocean in San Pedro, you'll find the biggest collection of Southern California marine life on exhibit anywhere. The **Cabrillo Marine Aquarium** (3720 Stephen M. White Dr., San Pedro; 310-548-7562; cabrillomarineaquarium .org) has many species of animals that live in and around the waters of Southern California. You can feel a slimy sea hare or a bumpy sea star along with many other sea creatures. Stop at the Exploration Center and get a worm's-eye view of the world. Check out the Aquatic Nursery where you can see baby and adult pipefish. They're cool because like sea horses, male pipefish carry and incubate eggs in a special pouch. Sign up for a Science at the Seashore Adventure to learn more about the California coastline and the creatures that inhabit the sea here. Have you ever seen a kelp forest? You can here. Kelp is the largest and fastest-growing seaweed—up to 2 feet a day! Many sea creatures call these forests home. You'll love the aquarium's Exploration Center where you can use microscopes in the Naturalists Corner or create artwork in the Discovery Center. Before you come, check out the aquarium website.

Talk Like a Surfer

When you surf, you ride on the forward face of a wave toward shore. It's harder than it looks! At least you can talk like a surfer! They have a language of their own.

A **gremmie** is a beginning surfer. He'd be **stoked** (very happy) to be on these beaches, but might end up **taking gas** (losing control). Surfers call really great waves **all time**. Here's some more surfer lingo:

Bail: To step off the board in order to avoid being knocked off.

Shoulder: The unbroken part of the wave.

Gnarly: Large, difficult waves.

Bomb: An exceptionally large wave.

Pop-Up: Going from lying on the board to sanding—in one jump!

Quiver: A surfer's collection of boards.

DID YOU KNOW?

Plastic kills sea creatures. They get entangled in discarded fishing lines or mistake plastic for food and choke on it. Pick up your trash and don't throw it in the water.

A VISITING KID SAYS:
"I love watching the surfers at the beach, but you have to get up early to see them."
—Kylee, 11, Little Rock, AR

Whale Watching

Look for the "blow." When a whale comes up to breathe, it sends a cloud of air and water up as high as 15 feet. Watch for blows 30 to 50 seconds apart.

Each winter, thousands of gray whales travel south from Alaska along California's coast to Baja, where they have their babies, and finally farther south. The 5,000-mile trip is the longest any mammal migrates each year. They travel in small groups fairly close to the shoreline. Each day they cover 70 to 80 miles, surfacing every few minutes to breathe. In the spring, they return with their new babies. The babies weigh more than 1,100 pounds and are 15 feet long.

You can try to spot the whales from shore. It's not easy. Or you can go out on a whale watching boat. Many of the beach towns—from Santa Barbara to San Pedro—offer such trips. Take one with the **Cabrillo Marine Aquarium** (3720 Stephen M. White Dr., San Pedro; 310-548-7562; cabrillomarine aquarium.org). If you're lucky, you'll see whales jump out of the water and then fall back in, making a huge splash. It's called breaching. Don't forget your binoculars.

DID YOU KNOW?

More than 70 percent of the earth's surface is covered by ocean.

TELL THE ADULTS:

Beaches and pools are lots of fun, but they can also be dangerous. The vast majority of drownings occur when children are not being supervised:

- Designate an adult to be a "water watcher." Take turns even if there's a lifeguard on duty. Adults should be "touching distance" to preschoolers and toddlers around the water. Don't rely on water wings or other inflatable toys either, pediatricians warn. They may give your child a false sense of security.

- Insist that older kids swim with a buddy. Remind them to stay away from pool and hot tub drains where they can get sucked under water.

- If visiting friends or relatives with a pool, make sure young children are carefully supervised at all times and that pool gates are locked.

- Don't let kids swim unsupervised—even if there's a lifeguard on duty. Parents should watch your younger brothers and sisters every second around the pool or ocean. Drowning is the leading cause of accidental death for young children in California.

- When boating, even if you're great swimmers, wear coast guard–approved life jackets.

9

Disneyland:

Mickey Mouse, Buzz Lightyear & Princess Power

It all started because Walt Disney

got tired of taking his kids to the merry-go-round. *There ought to be someplace better where parents and kids could have fun together,* he kept thinking.

That "someplace" became **Disneyland** (1313 Disneyland Railroad, Anaheim; 714-781-4565; disneyland.disney.go.com). After years of planning and dreaming, he opened the park in 1955 with just 18 attractions (the big pirate ship in Fantasyland was only half painted on opening day!). Disney had sunk all his money in the project. Few expected it to last.

Boy were they wrong! More than a half century later, Disneyland has entertained kings, athletes, astronauts, and celebrities from all over the world as well as tens of millions of parents and kids and was the inspiration for Walt Disney World in Florida and Disney Parks around the world.

Today there are some 60 major attractions spread out in 8 theme "lands" across 85 acres: Main Street, U.S.A., Adventureland, Critter Country, Frontierland, Fantasyland, Tomorrowland, New Orleans Square, and Mickey's Toontown.

Next door is **Disney California Adventure** (1313 S. Disneyland Dr., Anaheim; 714-781-4565; disneyland.disney .go.com/disneys-california-adventure), a theme park all about California that we'll get into in the next chapter.

A LOCAL KID SAYS:
"I always carry around a camera for pictures and money for souvenirs at a theme park."
—Guadalupe, 15

{ What's Cool? Mickey Mouse ears with your name on them. You can get them at the Mad Hatter in Fantasyland and on Main Street and the Gag Factory in Toontown, Tomorrowland, and elsewhere.

Whatever land you visit, you'll find some thrills, some laughs, and plenty of fun. The ghosts seem real at the Haunted Mansion, so do the animals—alligators among them—on the Jungle Cruise (check out those headhunters!).

Enter Fantasyland through Sleeping Beauty's Castle, where you can climb into bobsleds for a twisting ride through the Matterhorn's ice caverns—right into an alpine lake. Watch out for the Abominable

A LOCAL KID SAYS:
"I always have snacks in my backpack at a theme park."
—Amber, 12

What's Cool? Getting soaked on Splash Mountain on a hot day. Sit in the front of the log!

Snowman. Younger kids like to take Peter Pan's Flight to Never, Never Land. You'll meet Dumbo the Flying Elephant, Pinocchio, Snow White, and other characters from Disney animated films here. Nearby is a ride that everyone will love: It's a Small World. A small boat takes you around the world, as you are serenaded by hundreds of mechanized children and animals dressed in native costumes from dozens of countries.

DID YOU KNOW?

The first orange trees were planted in California in 1853. Orange County is named for the orange groves that have flourished there ever since.

Knott's Berry Farm really did start out as a farm growing berries.

If you like thrills, you'll love Splash Mountain in Critter Country where you race down the mountain in a log flume—dropping 5 stories into a pond as more than 100 characters like Brer Rabbit entertain you.

In New Orleans Square, you can head out on a voyage with the Pirates of the Caribbean and sail directly into battle. Visit the port as it's overtaken by drunken pirates—some of whom land in jail.

The cartoon stars moved to Mickey's Toontown, the story goes, to get away from Hollywood. Stop in and see Mickey Mouse at his house (Pluto's doghouse is in the garden). You'll find Mickey in his Movie Barn. Here's your chance to get his autograph or take a picture with him. Minnie lives next door in a

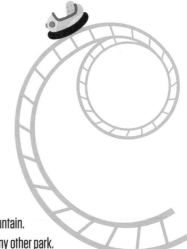

What's Cool? The coasters at Magic Mountain. There are more big ones than at just about any other park.

118

pink and purple house. Minnie will pose for pictures, too.

Roller-coaster fans won't be able to get enough of Space Mountain in Tomorrowland. It took more than a million hours to design and build the ride that blasts off and hurtles you through space—all in the dark. You also won't want to miss Buzz Lightyear Astro Blasters or Captain EO. It's a great show.

Another great roller coaster is Big Thunder Mountain Railroad in Frontierland, where you'll rock and roll through an underground earthquake. Take a break on Tom Sawyer Island in Frontierland and then figure out where to go next.

DID YOU KNOW?

A Disney employee is called a cast member; the people who design all of the fun attractions are Imagineers.

Who Was Walt Disney?

When Walt was a kid, he thought the clouds looked like animals. He grew up to be a talented cartoonist, and in 1928—more than 80 years ago—he created a cartoon mouse. His first movie was a black-and-white cartoon (no color in those days) called *Steamboat Willie,* and it was a huge success. He went on to make other famous animated movies. But Walt Disney had a problem. He'd take his daughters to amusement parks but couldn't find enough rides where he could have fun, too. So he decided to build a park where grown-ups could have fun along with kids. Disneyland opened in Anaheim in 1955 and was an immediate success. So many families loved it, he decided to build an even bigger park—Disney World in Orlando, Florida. He died before Disney World opened in 1971, but his brother Roy and all of the very talented people who worked for him made sure the Florida park was the way he would have wanted.

DID YOU KNOW?

Mickey Mouse was almost named Mortimer. Walt Disney's wife Lillian convinced him to go with Mickey instead.

Main Street, U.S.A. is partly based on Marceline, Missouri, where Walt Disney grew up.

FASTPASS

Want to skip the lines? So does everyone. That's why Disney created the FASTPASS for its most popular attractions. Here's how it works. You go to the FAST-PASS machine at the entrance to the attractions and put in your park ticket. You'll get another ticket with the time you should return when you can pretty much walk right in. While you're waiting, you can head to other attractions that don't have long lines, like Disneyland's Railroad, It's a Small World, or Tom Sawyer Island. Eat or shop while you're waiting instead of standing in a line. Just remember you can't get another FASTPASS for another attraction for a few hours (read the fine print on your ticket!). And make sure you get the FASTPASS for the attractions you most want to see early in the day because the numbers are limited and they will run out on busy days. You can see all the FASTPASS attractions on your map. Soon, you may be able to arrange to get a FASTPASS before you even arrive at the park. Disney is experimenting with new technology that will enable you to pre-load your FASTPASS at home for certain times.

DID YOU KNOW?

Tuesday, Wednesday, and Thursday are the least crowded days to visit Disneyland. Saturday is the busiest.

Autographs & Photos

Keep that autograph book handy! There are plenty of places to meet up with the characters at the parks, but sometimes, you'll have to wait in line for the opportunity. And sometimes, you get there just as the characters are leaving!

Some of the best spots are Toontown (Mickey, Minnie, Donald, Goofy, Pooh and Pals) and Fantasyland's Castle Fantasy Faire.

If you want to meet Mickey, go to his Toontown house—as soon as it opens!

A VISITING KID SAYS:
"Don't forget your autograph book. You get to show everyone at school, and it is a keepsake you can keep until you are grown up."
—Aubrei, 11, Decatur, IL

Tell your parents to check that day's guide map to see where your favorite characters will be. Another way to guarantee that you can meet and greet your favorites is to have your parents book a character meal. They come around to your table while you are eating to pose for pictures and sign autographs. Which characters do you most want to meet?

Princess Power!

The Magic Kingdom is where many of the Disney princesses live, and you can become one, too, with sparkles in your hair, tiaras, wands, and dresses or a "cool dude" prince at the Bibbidi Bobbidi Boutique. (Of course, this costs extra and you need reservations. It's in Cinderella's Castle.)

The Castle Couture shop sells everything princess, and you can get your picture taken here too. You'll see lots of little girls in the park in their favorite princess's dress—Belle, Jasmine, Mulan, Pocahontas, Tiana, Ariel, Aurora . . . who is your favorite princess?

DID YOU KNOW?

There are 10 Disney princesses. Snow White was the first. She made her debut in 1937 in *Snow White and the Seven Dwarfs*. Cinderella was the second in 1950.

At Castle Fantasy Faire, you can meet and great your favorite princesses throughout the day. Walk through Sleeping Beauty's Castle, which will tell you her story, and try your hands at Scottish games while waiting to meet Princess Merida.

If you want to eat with your favorite princesses, you can at Ariel's Grotto in Disney California Adventure. Make sure your parents make reservations by calling 714-781-3463.

Camp Snoopy & Monster Coasters

There are two other theme parks nearby that are popular with parents and kids—**Six Flags Magic Mountain** (26101 Magic Mountain Pkwy., Valencia; 661-255-4100; sixflags.com/magicmountain) and **Knott's Berry Farm** (8039 Beach Blvd., Buena Park; 714-220-5200; knotts.com). Adjacent to Knott's Berry Farm is a separate water park, too—**Soak City Orange County** (8039 Beach Blvd., Buena Park; 714-220-5200; soakcity oc.com).

Knott's Berry Farm is divided into areas representing differ-ent times in California history, from Ghost Town to Indian Trails, showcasing Native American crafts and culture. Fiesta Village

DID YOU KNOW?

The *Pirates of the Caribbean* movies were based on the attraction, not the other way around. This was the last ride that Walt Disney himself developed.

highlights California's Span-
ish heritage. The Boardwalk
celebrates Southern California beach towns, and Camp
Snoopy focuses on California's High
Sierra. Younger kids especially like Camp Snoopy with
more than 30 kid-size attractions. At Halloween, when Knott's
Berry Farm is known for its very scary Halloween Haunt, there's
also a Snoopy's Costume Party for younger kids.

If you like roller coasters, you'll love Boomerang. You're
turned upside down six times in less than a minute. If that's not
enough of a thrill, try Montezooma's Revenge where you zip
through a 76-foot loop frontward—and backward.

Six Flags Magic Mountain is about an hour and a half
from Anaheim and famous for roller coasters. It is best for kids
over 42 inches tall, though there are some shows and rides for
younger kids, including the **Hurricane Harbor** water park
next door (26101 Magic Mountain Pkwy., Valencia; 661-255-4527;
sixflags.com/hurricaneharborla). If you love coasters, you'll love
Magic Mountain's attractions—including *five* water rides.

Take your pick of the Apocalypse, Full Throttle, Scrambler,
Road Runner Express, Tatsu, and more.

TELL THE ADULTS:

It's often tough to eat healthy at theme parks, but Disney is making that easier. Kids' meals now include a healthy side of fruit or veggies and a choice of lowfat milk, juice, or water rather than a sugary drink. Toddler meals are also available in some places. If you don't see a kids' menu, just ask!

- Californians who visit all the time often brown-bag it for lunch or dinner. It's cheaper and saves time! Always pack reusable water bottles and snacks.

- There are a lot of restaurants just outside the parks in Downtown Disney, whether you want pizza, a sandwich, or to eat amid monkeys in a tropical rain forest at the Rainforest Cafe (1515 Disneyland Dr., Anaheim; 714-772-0413; rainforestcafe.com).

- Especially if you want a character meal or a sit-down meal within the theme parks, it's smart to make a reservation ahead of time. (You can book up to 60 days in advance at 714-781-3463.)

- Downtown Disney is a great place to shop—and trade pins—as the shops open early and close late.

- You can also de-stress the experience by staying overnight at one of the Disney hotels so you can take advantage of early admission to the parks, take a break during the day for a swim—and a nap—and easily return in the evening for the fireworks.

- Visit disneyland.disney.go.com for the latest deals on the three Disneyland Resort Hotels with their themed meals, amenities, and decor. Free transportation to and from the parks is available via monorails and trams and buses to neighboring hotels. There are more than 40 properties nearby known as Disneyland Good Neighbor hotels. Visit the Anaheim/Orange County Visitor and Convention Bureau at anaheimoc.org and go to "deals and discounts" or call 714-765-8888.

- To further de-stress your theme park experience, take a virtual tour with the kids at disneyland .com before you visit and make sure everyone gets a pick each day of their "top attraction." Alternate whose attraction goes first each day!

10

Disney California Adventure:

Coasters, Hang Gliding & Radiator Springs

Ready to race?

Radiator Springs Racers at **Disney California Adventure** (1313 S. Disneyland Dr., Anaheim; 714-781-4565; disney land.disney.go.com/disneys-california-adventure) is every-one's new favorite ride. You really will feel like you are in "the cutest little town in Carburetor Country" where all the characters of the *Cars* movies live.

California Adventure has some of the Disneyland Resort's most popular attractions. You'll love **Soarin' Over California,** which makes you feel as if you are hang gliding over the state—from Yosemite Falls to an aircraft carrier in San Diego Bay to San Francisco's Golden Gate Bridge.

Everything in this park is themed after California, from the entrance designed to look like 1920s LA when Walt

DID YOU KNOW?

You can draw your own favorite character and learn how animation works at Disney Animation and the Animation Academy at Disney California Adventure.

The Tower of Terror building is 199 feet tall. Get ready to drop 13 stories . . .

Disney arrived to Hollywoodland to Paradise Pier, which is supposed to make you think of old-fashioned California seaside boardwalks, to Grizzly Peak, an 8-acre mini wilderness like Northern California's redwood country.

Coaster lovers give a thumbs up to **California Screamin'**, the centerpiece of Paradise Pier. It's designed to look like an old-fashioned wooden coaster, but the thrills are all 21st century. The cars go from zero to 55 miles per hour in less than 5 seconds!

A VISITING KID SAYS:
"Be brave and try everything because you don't know what you'll like or when you will be back."
—Emily, 14, Arizona

A VISITING KID SAYS:
"I liked Soarin' Over California. It is really realistic, and you'll feel like you are really hang gliding."
—Marie Claire, 13, Arkansas

{ What's Cool? Beating your parents' score at Toy Story Midway Mania!

We can't forget **The Twilight Zone Tower of Terror.**
According to legend, lightning struck the building on
Halloween night 1939, and an entire guest wing disappeared—along with an elevator carrying five people. Are
you ready for the biggest drop of your life?

Of course, every ride at California Adventure isn't
scary! If you want to get wet,
head for **Grizzly River
Run.** Check out the
mining relics scat-
tered about and get
ready to get drenched
on your raft.

A VISITING KID SAYS:
"Radiator Springs Racers was really
fun. You feel like you are in the
movie at Cars Land."
—Trevor, 12, Arizona

Everyone loves **Toy
Story Midway Mania!**
You wear 3-D glasses and try
to see how many points you can score on the animated

DID YOU KNOW?

Pacific Wharf at Disney
California Adventure is
inspired by Monterey,
California. Taste fresh-baked
sourdough bread on the
Bakery Tour.

targets. You are inside the Midway. It is really cool! And when you are done, check out the Paradise Pier Midway with plenty of games.

At **Turtle Talk with Crush,** everyone's favorite cartoon turtle actually talks to you, answering questions. Even if you don't watch the Muppets anymore on TV, you'll laugh along with them at **Muppet Vision 3-D** hosted by Gonzo. You won't want to miss the It's Tough to be a Bug Show either with plenty of creepy-crawlies and 4-D effects.

Cars Land is the newest addition to California Adventure complete with a 525-foot-long Route 66. Stop for a shake at Flo's V8 Cafe and check out all the neon lights after dark. Board one of Luigi's flying tires (think bumper cars meet flying saucers), and then get ready to compete against other race cars as you drive through Ornament Valley, meeting the *Cars* crew along the way. Wow! That was some hairpin turn!

{ **What's Cool?** Posing for a photo in front of Walt Disney's statue with Mickey Mouse.

DID YOU KNOW?

Many kids don't realize Walt Disney was a real person.

The entrance to Disney California Adventure is Buena Vista Street, which is designed to look like the Los Angeles Walt Disney saw when he first arrived in 1923. He was just 22 years old and had just $40 in his pocket.

Pin Mania!

Wherever you go at Disney California Adventure, you'll see adults and kids wearing lanyards around their necks that are covered with shiny pins. There are hundreds of different ones! You can buy a pin to commemorate your birthday or your favorite ride, character, or Disney movie (disneystore.com). There are light-up pins, pins that spin, and 3-D pins.

The Walt Disney Company has always offered collectible Disney pins. During the Millennium Celebration in 1999, they encouraged guests to trade pins, and today, many grown-ups and kids do at the parks and even on eBay.

Want to start trading? Find a Disney pin you like and look for a Disney cast member wearing a pin lanyard. They're ready to trade!

Holidays with Mickey

It seems Mickey and Minnie are always celebrating something. Some of the most fun celebrations—besides your own birthday, of course:

- **Fourth Of July:** Celebrate Independence Day with especially cool fireworks.

- **Halloween:** At Disneyland, Halloween Time lets you celebrate in not-too-scary ways with special shows, fireworks, and Mickey's Halloween Party.

- **Christmas:** By early November, you'll see the holiday decorations on Main Street. There's a special holiday-themed fireworks show, A Christmas Fantasy parade, and more.

Staying Safe

Theme parks are big places. Set up a meeting place just in case some of you get separated. Have your parents write down the name of your hotel, the phone number, and their cell phone numbers in case you get separated (sure you know their cell number—but in case you forget). If you do get separated from your parents, look for someone in a Disney uniform. They can help you find your family!

Put your name and contact numbers on your cameras and backpacks. Disney does a great job of returning lost items.

And don't try to stand on tiptoes to meet the height requirements of a ride. They are there for a reason—to keep you safe!

What's Cool? Watching the nighttime water and lights show World of Color waterside. There are 1,200 fountains. Get there 45 minutes ahead of time for a good spot!

- If anyone in the family has special needs or challenges, Disney California Adventure has a special Guide Map for Guests with Disabilities, special handheld devices that verbally describe the parks, and assistive listening devices as well as special accommodations for those with autism and other challenges (disneyland.disney.go.com/plan/guest-services/guests-with-disabilities).

DID YOU KNOW?

When refrigerated railroad cars were invented, California-grown fruits and vegetables began to be shipped to the rest of the US. Today California is an agricultural giant producing more than 200 kinds of fruits and vegetables including walnuts, oranges, asparagus, almonds, broccoli, and dates.

- Toy Story Midway Mania! and Soarin' Over California have particularly devoted fans. Get to the park early and get to these attractions first to take advantage of the FASTPASS system whenever you can to avoid waiting in line.

There is also a lot of entertainment at the park that won't require waits:

- Buena Vista News Boys where Mickey Mouse joins the fun at the Buena Vista Street's Red Car Trolley.

- Phineas and Ferb's Rockin' Rollin' Dance Party where you can dance along.

- Pixar Play Parade.

- World of Color 25-minute night show of music animation and special effects all over water.

- Many of the park's attractions have height restrictions. They are there to keep kids safe so no standing on tiptoes! The rides will be here when the kids are taller.

ADVENTURE SCAVENGER HUNT

Look carefully in the park for all the following and check off what you find!

- ❑ The Golden Gate Bridge

- ❑ Yosemite

- ❑ California Screamin'

- ❑ Tower of Terror

- ❑ Grizzly River Run

- ❑ Woody and Buzz

- ❑ Crush

- ❑ Kermit

- ❑ Bugs

- ❑ Minnie Mouse

- ❑ Someone wearing a lanyard with shiny pins

- ❑ Someone winning a game in the Midway

- ❑ A replica of Walt Disney

- ❑ Lightning McQueen

- ❑ Paradise Pier

- ❑ A visitor taking a silly picture

Use the space below to collect signatures of any celebrities or Disney characters you might see.

Use the space below to draw pictures of any celebrities or Disney characters you might see.

What a Trip!

I came to Los Angeles with:

_____

_____

_____

The weather was:

_____

_____

_____

We went to:

_____

_____

_____

We ate:

_____

_____

_____

We bought:

_____

_____

_____

I saw these famous LA sites:

_____

_____

_____

My favorite thing about LA was:

_____

_____

_____

My best memory of LA was:

_____

_____

_____

My favorite souvenir is:

_____

_____

_____

You had such a great time in Los Angeles! Draw some pictures or paste in some photos of your trip!

Index

Answer Keys

LA Word Search (p. 41)

S	W	L	D	R	P	X	W	F	U	N	F	V
A	U	A	B	V	A	S	U	N	S	E	T	O
B	M	B	M	R	C	O	A	R	E	G	A	A
E	T	R	R	B	I	E	B	I	L	E	R	L
R	P	E	C	I	F	A	C	M	A	T	A	N
T	S	A	N	L	I	F	Q	R	R	T	T	F
O	I	T	Q	L	C	R	I	V	P	Y	H	O
O	D	A	Z	B	O	N	O	M	N	C	E	S
T	N	R	Y	O	C	C	J	A	R	E	G	S
H	L	P	M	A	E	K	O	S	M	N	R	I
Y	F	I	O	R	A	H	L	R	E	T	O	L
J	U	T	R	D	N	Q	X	T	K	E	V	S
E	C	S	M	S	N	R	S	E	W	R	E	N
S	A	N	T	A	M	O	N	I	C	A	B	C

Secret Word Puzzle (p. 56)

Hollywood Walk of Fame

Sports Word Scramble (p. 71)

ANGELS (Baseball)

CLIPPERS (Men's Basketball)

DODGERS (Baseball)

DUCKS (Hockey)
GALAXY (Soccer)
KINGS (Hockey)
LAKERS (Men's Basketball)
SPARKS (Women's Basketball)

Where is a fun place to visit right on the beach? (p. 99)
Dogtown
Pacific Park
Venice
Gray whales
Santa Barbara
Channel Islands
Muscle Beach
Andree Clark Bird Reserve
International Chess Park
Bird Refuge
Carpinteria
Lifeguards
Stearns Wharf
J. Paul Getty Villa

Answer: Santa Monica Pier

About the Author

Award-winning author Eileen Ogintz is a leading national family travel expert whose syndicated Taking the Kids is the most widely distributed column in the country on family travel. She has also created TakingtheKids.com, which helps families make the most of their vacations together. Ogintz is the author of seven family travel books and is often quoted in major publications such as *USA Today*, the *Wall Street Journal*, and the *New York Times*, as well as parenting and women's magazines on family travel. She has appeared on such television programs as *The Today Show*, *Good Morning America*, and *The Oprah Winfrey Show*, as well as dozens of local radio and television news programs. She has traveled around the world with her three children and others in the family, talking to traveling families wherever she goes. She is also the author of *The Kid's Guide to New York City*, *The Kid's Guide to Orlando*, *The Kid's Guide to Washington, DC*, and *The Kid's Guide to Chicago* (Globe Pequot Press).